For the Islands I Sing

George Mackay Brown wrote this beautiful and touching book in the years before his death in 1996, but he did not want it published while he lived. In it his simple, bardic honesty is turned upon himself.

George's memory is inseparable from Orkney, where he was born the youngest child of a poor family and which he rarely left. His mother was a beauty from the north coast of Scotland who spoke only Gaelic until she went to school. His father John doubled as postman and tailor. John was a wit, mimic and singer privately given to worry and doubt, and a gentle radical who told his children 'Whatever happens, keep humble.'

Tuberculosis framed George's early life. It kept him in a kind of limbo where nothing much was expected of him. In this 'desert of time' he discovered alcohol, which gave him an 'insight into the workings of the mind: how under the drab surface complexities there exists a ritualistically simple world of joy and anger'. He also began to write, both poems and stories. Edwin Muir invited him to study at Newbattle Abbey, where he learned more of literature and from where he went on to the University of Edinburgh. It was in that city that he came to know other poets, like Sydney Goodsir Smith, Hugh MacDiarmid and Norman McCaig – and Stella Cartwright with whom perhaps all of them were in love.

But it was back in Orkney that, in Seamus Heaney's words, 'his sense of the world and his way with words [became] powerfully at one with each other'. His themes were complex and universal but his voice shared the timeless simplicity of the islands and sea, and of the patterns of life so long part of them. As Peter Levi wrote, 'he gave one hope for poetry and the language', and his genius was celebrated by other artists also, especially perhaps Peter Maxwell Davies, so much of whose music sets his words. By the time of his death in 1996 he was recognized as one of the great writers of his time and country.

For the Islands I Sing

An Autobiography

❖ ❖ ❖

GEORGE MACKAY BROWN

JOHN MURRAY
Albemarle Street, London

© The Estate of George Mackay Brown 1997

First published in 1997
by John Murray (Publishers) Ltd,
50 Albemarle Street, London W1X 4BD

Hardback reprinted twice 1997

First published in paperback in 1998
Reprinted 1998 (twice)

A catalogue record for this book is available from the British Library

HBK ISBN 0-7195-5628 7
PBK ISBN 0-7195-5889 1

Typeset in Monophoto Sabon

Printed and bound in Great Britain by
The University Press, Cambridge

For the
Islands I Sing

✧ ✧ ✧

The Orkney islands lie to the north of Scotland, sundered by what is often a stormy piece of water, the Pentland Firth. The tides huddle herds-long – the Atlantic pouring into the North Sea, and North Sea into Atlantic four times a day. If there are contrary winds, tremendous seas can build up.

Those islands, and the Shetlands further to the northeast, have a strange history. They have been inhabited continuously for more than 5,000 years, and the stone farms and villages and burial chambers are witness to an ancient lineage. Orkney was part of Pictland in the early centuries AD. A great change took place in the fortunes of the islands when Vikings from Scandinavia opened marauding and trade and settlement routes westward a few centuries later. From then on the history of the islands was written down in a wonderful piece of literature called *Orkneyinga Saga*; before that, all is guesswork and speculation. Successive earls of Orkney – some violent, some able, some weak – like rulers everywhere – were vassals of the King of Norway. Under Earl Thorfinn ('the mighty') who ruled from Birsay in Orkney, were – we are told – nine Scottish earldoms. At that time, the eleventh century, the Earl of Orkney was at least as powerful as the King of Scotland. Earl Thorfinn and the much maligned Macbeth were probably cousins; already ties were being made between Orkney and Scotland; as Scotland became stronger and more united, Orkney was increasingly drawn away from Norway into the Scottish orbit. In 1263 King Hakon of Norway made a last effort to maintain a hold over the islands in the west. His fleet sailed from Scapa and was defeated at Largs in south-west Scotland, as much by adverse weather as by the Scots. The broken king, on his way home, died in Kirkwall in Orkney that winter.

The most intriguing part of *Orkneyinga Saga* concerns the struggle of two cousins, Hakon and Magnus, for the earldom of Orkney. Often the earldom had two claimants, a state of affairs that seems to have been encouraged by the overlord in Norway, because Orkney under a single strong earl was semi-independent; but two claimants allowed the king to play one off against the other. Hakon and Magnus agreed to hold a peace conference on the island of Egilsay on Easter Monday, 1117. Magnus sailed there with a few advisers and the stipulated number of ships: two. Hakon sailed in with eight ships full of warmen, clamouring for the death of Earl Magnus. Magnus spent that night in the church of Egilsay ('the church island'), and in the morning he went out to meet Hakon 'as cheerfully as though he was bidden to a feast'. Preparations were made for the execution of Magnus. Hakon told his standard-bearer to do the killing. This man, Ofeig, 'refused indignantly'. None of Hakon's followers, it seemed, was willing to do such a thing on Easter Monday. At last the axe was put into the hands of Earl Hakon's cook, a man called Lifolf. And Lifolf, when he knew what he had to do, began to weep. At this point Magnus encouraged his executioner, pointing out that his own rich clothes would be Lifolf's, and absolving him from all blame. Then, weeping, Lifolf drove the great axe into Magnus' head. Hakon thereafter was sole Earl of Orkney.

Such a villainous piece of work should have suffered nemesis, according to our way of thinking since the Greeks gave us tragedy. But in fact Earl Hakon went on to become one of the best earls Orkney ever had, much loved and popular with the islanders.

At a level deeper than politics, the murder of Earl Magnus began its operations. Almost at once the common people looked on the dead man as a saint. It was not murder but martyrdom. People sick in mind and body began to flock to Magnus' tomb in Birsay, and extraordinary cures were reported. At first William, Bishop of Orkney, disapproved of such vulgar credulity, but later his eyes were opened – literally and metaphorically – to the presence of something rare and strange and new in the life of the islands; a sweetness and light unknown before. The bones of Magnus were taken to the new cathedral that was being built in Kirkwall, and immured in a pillar there. They are there, cloven skull and bone, today.

These historical events form the backdrop to much of the narrative and verse that I have written. Without the violent beauty of those happenings eight and a half centuries ago, my writing would have been quite different. (I was almost going to say, it would not have existed; but of course the talent that will not let one rest would have had to latch on to other themes. There are, fortunately for me, many legendary and historical sources in Orkney from

later centuries that any native-born writer can seize on
with delight – but still the great story of Magnus and
Hakon is the cornerstone.)

I will mention one other magnificent episode from
Orkneyinga Saga which has provided more good stone for
the building, and that is the crusade to Jerusalem,
Byzantium, and Rome undertaken by the nephew of Saint
Magnus, Earl Rognvald Kolson, between 1151 and 1154. It
was not so much a crusade as a pilgrimage, a kind of penitential voyage, but the old Viking spirit was still so active
in the fifteen ships that sailed into the Mediterranean that
they besieged and burned down a castle in Spain, made a
piratical assault on a peaceful Moslem merchant ship, and
spent months in the French seaport of Narbonne where
Earl Rognvald fell in love with Ermengarde the Countess.
At last he managed to tear himself away, but his mouth and
harp sounded the praises of Ermengarde everywhere in the
inland sea. It is interesting to note how gradually the name
of the loved one lessens and vanishes at last from his verses.
By the time the pilgrim ships reached Acre the lyrics have
stopped.

That same Earl Rognvald Kolson, as the writer of
Orkneyinga Saga portrays him, is a remarkable man. He
was one of those who accomplish with ease and grace all
that they turn their hand to – politics, war, poetry, court-
ship. But apart from aristocratic pursuits, he could fish in
stormy seas, ski in the Norwegian mountains, wield a
hammer in the smithy. Those humbler accomplishments
must have endeared him to the common people. After his
death in Caithness they called him Saint Rognvald; but

there is no record of any cure at his shrine. Perhaps he delighted too much in the things of this present world to have arrived at the essence of sanctity that the life of Magnus distilled. But the pages that record his doings breathe sweetness and fragrance; here, under all that wealth of talent and achievement, beat the pulses of a good man.

✧ ✧ ✧

Something should be said about the islands themselves. The group consists of one large island, called 'the horse island', Hrossey, by the Vikings; but somewhere at the time of map-making a pedantic hand wrote 'Mainland' on the parchment, and so it is insipidly called today. There is a cluster of smaller islands to the north of Mainland, and a cluster to the south: those southern islands, with Mainland itself, enclose the harbourage of Scapa Flow, famous in two world wars.

The Orkneys are not barren like so much of the adjacent Highlands of Scotland. They are beautifully shaped islands, little green and brown hills rising out of the sea, or low green islands fringed with sand beaches. They have been cultivated for millennia, and the green of tilth and pasture has spread with the toil of generations until now the islands seem to wear coats of fertility. There are good farms everywhere, and on market days the farmers drive into the two towns, Kirkwall (the capital) and Stromness. Farming is relatively prosperous now, but in former generations most of the little farmers and the crofters had to eke out their living from the sea. Nowadays fishermen special-ise in their own trade, and with their new bigger boats and modern gear get much richer harvests from the sea than their forefathers did.

I mention farmers and fishermen because they figure so largely in the stories and poems I have written. The two rhythms of land and sea I have tried to weave into my work; they are, in one sense, different and opposed, and yet, once taken into the imagination, they beget a pattern and a harmony.

The centuries have thrown up other classes and charac-ters: the lairds (or landlords), merchants, ministers, lawyers and skippers. All have left their mark on the life of the islands. And of course they varied as individuals. A bad laird could cause much misery to his tenants; a good laird could be a kind of father to his people.

The Presbyterian ministry has, over four centuries, pro-duced a great crop of eccentric and learned men. Many of them added a special flavour to the parish or island they resided in. A few have passed into legend.

✧ ✧ ✧

I was born in the town of Stromness, on the main island of Orkney, in October 1921.

Stromness is a newer town than Kirkwall, whose roots are in the Middle Ages. Stromness grew from what I imagine must have been a group of fishermen's huts in the late sixteenth century; then a man called William Clark built an inn on the north shore of the bay. He and his wife Mareon would not have built an inn for small farmers and fishermen. There must have been the first stirrings of trade, with bigger ships sailing to Scandinavia and the Baltic, and even beginning to seek west to the American colonies. Stromness – called by the Vikings Hamnavoe, which means 'haven inside the bay' – has a fine natural harbour, sheltered from the west by a steep hill called Brinkie's Brae and from the east by two little tidal islands, the Holms. In times of storm, which can break out at any season of the year, Stromness was a good place of refuge. The village grew rapidly in the eighteenth century, when the constant wars with the French made it safer to sail round the north of Scotland than through the English Channel. Orkneymen – lairds' sons, probably – began to build their own ships and to trade with the northern European ports. The little town is much the same now as it must have been 200 years ago – except for modern munici- pal building schemes that fringe the town, and look out of place alongside the long helter-skelter of houses that form the nucleus. The early town was built to no plan, and out of no aesthetic impulse, but by some stroke of chance what emerged was, and remains, beautiful. The houses on the upper side are built into the steep granite-studded hill; on the seaward side they are built on stone piers that jut out into the harbour water. The old Stromness is a ballad in stone. Much younger than its neighbour and rival, Kirkwall, it keeps its own legends and lore, most of them sea-salted. It nurtured an eighteenth-century pirate called

John Gow, and less than a generation later a heroic merchant called Alexander Graham who ruined himself fighting to rid Stromness of the tax imposed by Kirkwall on such as himself for the privilege of trading (a right which belonged to the 'royal burghs' of Scotland only). And the great romantic poet and novelist Sir Walter Scott, in 1814, hobbled up the steep brae – he being cripple – to talk with nonagenarian Bessie Millie, a kind of spaewife who sold favourable winds to storm-bound mariners for sixpence a time. Partly from what she told him, Scott wrote his novel of Orkney and Shetland called *The Pirate*. (As a small girl, Bessie Millie had seen Gow and his ruffians strutting on the waterfront.)

Stromness grew, and prospered. In the nineteenth century it was the centre for recruiting young men for the Hudson's Bay Company in Canada, and for the whaling in the Davis Straits. Many of those young Orkneymen settled in Canada and rose to high positions under the British Crown; others returned home, moderately affluent, and bought houses and farms. There were minglings of Orcadian and Indian blood. Money flowed through the merchants' coffers of Stromness, 'sweat of silver'. There remained always the poor, the fishermen who set lobster-creels under the high cliffs westward, and the hinterland crofters with a cow and a few sheep and an oatfield and a peatbank.

The little town, a-surge on the crest of progress, was stranded high and dry by the next wave. With the coming of steam-ships Stromness ceased to be so important; those new ugly vessels could ride out storms without resorting to the 'haven inside the bay'. The merchants' money-boxes ceased to rattle so loudly or so frequently. Stromness, after a boisterous youth, sank prematurely into a silver-gray age. It kept, still, a distillery and boat-building yards, but the strong pulse was out of it. The faithful fishermen still sailed in their frail boats along the Atlantic fringes. The farmers and their wives still came in to town, to the mart, on Wednesdays. Once or twice, about the turn of the century, the town was shaken with a sudden wealth of herring, and the long twisting street was full of Scottish herring-men and Gaelic girls employed to gut and salt the fish. But the herring, silver migrant droves, shifted their ground; and Stromness was old and gray and full of sleep.

About the time I was born, the distillery put up its shutters, and the hammers in the boatyard were falling silent. There had been so much riotous behaviour by marines and Irish 'navvies' in the First World War – such blood and beer spilt on the streets! – that the inhabitants indignantly voted the town 'dry'. All the taverns of Stromness had to close their doors, for a quarter of a century. The salt-throated men of Stromness – mostly fishermen – took their thirsts to country inns seven or eight miles away, by motor coach.

It was a very depressed little community that I was born into.

I have dwelt at some length on this background, because it is the setting to nearly all that I have written.

Orkney is a rich breeding ground for narrative and poetry. Two Orkneymen of a generation before me – Edwin Muir the poet and translator and essayist, and Eric Linklater the novelist – had tapped those sources, each in his own way. A lyric poet not so well-known, because his best work was written in the Orkney dialect, was Robert Rendall. It is possible, I sometimes think, that a dozen or so of his perfect lyrics will outlast all that we have done.

✧ ✧ ✧

I was the last child of a poor family. My father, John Brown, was a tailor; but the same 'progress' that had taken the wind out of sailing ships had hurt the tailors' trade. Suits were ready-made by machines in the cities of the south. So my father found only part-time work as a tailor. His main occupation was as a postman. It is in his postman's uniform that I chiefly remember him. The Orkney mail came across the Pentland Firth every afternoon on the mail-steamer *St Ola*. After the letters had been sorted by four or five postmen in the post office, my father set off on his round. I have one image of him, on what must have been a night of winter storm, coming into our kitchen–living room at Clouston's pier, the rain streaming off him. He had possibly come in to trim the lantern that every postman had, pinned to the lapel of the overcoat, to read the names and addresses on winter nights. Then he went once more into the tempest.

The Orkney weather, especially in winter, is full of 'wildness and wet'. A few hundreds of such soakings probably brought on the arthritis that crippled him in his fifties. Still, between bouts of illness when he had to keep to his bed, he struggled on with his postal round. But in the end it was too much for him. Thereafter he sat for a few hours every day in Peter Esson's tailor shop, cutting and stitching. Even that must have been painful for him, for the arthritis had twisted his hands.

He was a man of wit and humour. He had a way of saying things that made people laugh heartily and unrestrainedly. 'Jack Broon, it does me good to hear thee,' more than one old woman would say, as he left a letter in her hand and went on. He was a good mimic, and could imitate the voices of all the local eccentrics and 'characters'. He had a good tenor voice and loved to sing, especially about the New Year when the whisky was flowing; Edwardian music-hall songs and sentimental hymns were his favourites.

I think he had the makings of a good actor.

To the Stromness folk, he was a cheerful man who could turn anything to laughter. But there was a melancholy strain in him; once or twice, as a child, I listened outside the door of his bedroom where he paced back and fore, uttering aloud his doubts and worries. Those soliloquys put a kind of wonder and disquiet on me. Perhaps I was beginning to realise that human beings are much more complex than they seem to be. We put on masks when we go out of our houses into the community. Communal life is complex; we have a different mask for everyone we encounter. When there are four or five people in a group, the communication between them, however seemingly simple, can be very subtle. These mysteries I did not forget when I began to write fiction. In all human intercourse there are complex interweavings, like instruments in a quartet or a full orchestra. (Violin or flute by itself makes a very different music.)

There were very few books in our house – I remember *From Log Cabin to White House*. But my father, especially when he was ill, read extensively from books borrowed from the public library. He had a deep sympathy with the very poor of the urban slums. Books like Jack London's *People of the Abyss*, and Robert Tressell's *Ragged-Trousered Philanthropist*, and Patrick MacGill's *The Rat-Pit* and *Children of the Dead End*, impressed him very much. He was always on the side of the poor against the wealthy and over-privileged. I suppose, if he had been driven to define his political stance, he would have called himself a socialist, but a socialist of the Keir Hardie school; Marxism would have been a meaningless cold abstraction to him.

One of his great heroes was William Booth, the founder of the Salvation Army. Twice in one day, in Glasgow, when he must have been a young unmarried man, he heard Booth preaching to a huge concourse. Apart from the deep impression those sermons made on him, he remembered the day because, among the shifting throngs of listeners, on both occasions he found himself sitting next to the same stranger.

My father's elder brother, Peter, became an officer in the Salvation Army, and later a Congregational minister.

Every Sunday my father led the whole family, seven in all, to one of the three Presbyterian churches in our small town. He had no high regard, in general, for ministers or elders. But he sang the hymns and psalms, full-throated, from the very back seat of the gallery where we always sat, one foot on the seat and with the trouser leg hitched up so that a length of his drawers showed – a thing that caused me deep embarrassment.

And, three or four times during the long sermon, my mother passed along the row a paper bag of sweets. I loved the 'sweeties', but the rustling of the bag sounded like a small electric storm in the pauses of the minister's discourse – and that embarrassed me too, for I was sure that all the congregation must be listening to that paper bag and disapproving.

The Browns in Orkney are mainly concentrated in the parishes of Stromness and Sandwick. Many of the Orkney surnames are Norse, but not the Browns. It is a common Scottish name; almost certainly the first Browns came to Orkney in the sixteenth century or later, when the Scots moved into the islands in considerable numbers after Orkney became part of the Kingdom of Scotland in 1472. Judging from the old records, they were a fairly important family in the area for a century or two: farmers and merchants. There is a farm Brownstown on the south side of Brinkie's Brae, with a well at the roadside once reputed for its healing waters. (Such a well is a recurrent symbol in my writing.) A large area just south of the town was called Brownsquoy; there a Brown of some local standing must have had his house and fields. There were so many families called Brown in Stromness four or five generations ago that they had to be differentiated by pre-names. There were the 'Melvin Browns', who must have had property in the vicinity of the present-day Melvin Place. My ancestors were known as the 'Duckie Browns' because they kept ducks round a pond – long since filled in – near the foot of Hellihole Road. (The name Hellihole takes smiles to the faces of tourists, and they tilt their cameras to the name-plate on the wall of the public library: but helli-hole is possibly a corruption of 'holy-well', the healing well that is on Brownstown land.) The Duckie Browns were probably a poor branch of the family. At any rate, my father's father was a cobbler who lived in Brown's Close at the South End. I turned an old *Orkney Herald* file one day and discovered that, soon after the Education Act of 1872, my grandfather was taken to court and fined ten shillings for not sending his children to school. One day in the pub I heard an old fisherman say that the cobbler grandfather went on drinking sprees that lasted for a few days; he dressed up in his best clothes and sallied out to the ale-houses; when his thirst was satisfied, or his money was all gone, he returned to the worn boots, the rolls of leather, and the last . . .

The Browns have played their part in Scottish literature. There was the nineteenth-century essayist Dr John Brown. The best Scottish novel of the twentieth century was written by a young man called George Douglas Brown, the illegitimate son of an Ayrshire farmer: *The House with the Green Shutters*. Robert Burns's mother was called Agnes Brown; it was from that side of the family that the poet inherited his gift . . .

Family trees are so enormously complex that it is facile and dangerous to attach very much importance to a surname. So, though my name is Brown, I have such a

multitude of ancestors that only one-thousandth or one-
ten-thousandth of me is truly Brown, and even then there
is no definite certainty about it. Still, I fondly linger over
the notion that a drop of two of the same blood that
powered *Green Shutters* and *The Jolly Beggars* is in my
veins too. But it is not likely.

✧ ✧ ✧

My mother did not belong to the islands. She was one of
the nine children of a crofter–fisherman from Strathy in
Sutherland, on the north coast of Scotland. It is likely that
her near Mackay ancestors had had to endure the 'clear-
ances' of the early nineteenth century, when whole com-
munities of Gaelic-speaking Highlanders were persuaded
or driven out of the valleys where they had lived, a poor but
free community under the chiefs of Mackay, for many centuries. Again, it was 'progress', that religion of nineteenth-
century man − that irresistible force − that destroyed and
uprooted everything that seemed to stand in its way.
Nothing was sacred or beautiful; only money and profits
counted. The ancient way of life of the Scottish Gaels was
destroyed with particular ferocity − hadn't those clans
twice in the eighteenth century threatened the crown and
the ruling classes in England; and indeed, under Prince
Charles Edward Stuart, caused a wild panic in London's
corridors of power, in 1745? The Mackays had not
marched with the prince, but they were cut from the same
cloth: and it was high time for them to be gathered into the

'pax Britannica', or to be forced overseas. The clan chief was no longer the clan's protector; he had long sided with the establishment, and sent his sons to English public schools and married among the English or Lowland aristocracy. And it had been pointed out to him that it would be more profitable for him to graze flocks of Cheviot sheep on his lands than have them tilled in the age-old unhurried rhythms.

It must have been a poor living that the Mackays wrung out of the straths, but life for them was enriched by poetry and legend and song as old as Homer perhaps.

The roofs of the scattered clan were burned over their heads, the old and the sick were left to wander or die among the rocks. Those who were not forced on to ships Canada-bound were permitted to scratch a living from soil at the sea-edge northwards. The fishing, it was pointed out to them, was good. It is more than likely that hundreds of them had never even set eyes on the sea. Somehow they learned to be boatbuilders and fishermen. Somehow they learned to read the ferocious and fruitful moods of the Pentland Firth.

My mother was born in a little croft, in a hamlet called Braal, in 1891.

In that small house, and all over the north and west of Scotland, Gaelic was spoken. The only two words my mother knew of English at the time she went to school were 'yes' and 'no'. It seems to have been the official policy then to discourage, if not to extinguish altogether, the Gaelic language. Always, throughout history, there has been a bitterness and rancour between the Celts of Ireland and

Scotland and the Anglo-Saxons. There seems to be, still, an almost total lack of sympathy and neighbourliness. At the Strathy school, my mother and all the boys and girls had to learn English as fast and as well as they could manage. They were punished if the schoolmaster – I seem to remember, he was an Englishman – heard the pupils converse in Gaelic, even in the playground. So, the Highlanders grew up bilingual: but the subtly insinuated suggestions, repeated over and over, that English was the language of authority and business and the ascendancy, tore Gaelic to tatters in a few generations. That is to say, a whole rich culture was all but destroyed. Of course there were Celts who saw the peril. Nowadays – and perhaps for the past two generations – a stand is being made against the destruction of Gaelic culture, and perhaps something may be saved from the ruins. Or perhaps the continual erosion will, in the end, prove too much.

The Gaels of Scotland were so poor that large-scale emigration to America and the British colonies continued generation after generation. The glens emptied: the clans were scattered. My mother had to leave home too, in her mid teens. She came to work as a waitress in the large new-built hotel in Stromness, the proprietor of which was a Mackay and a distant relative of hers. Having been brought up in one of the strictest Calvinist sects, the Free Presbyterians, she thought that her stay in the Orkneys would last only a few days, because one of the first things she was told was that she would have to work on Sundays, and, among the Free Presbyterians, work on 'the Sabbath' is strictly forbidden. However, after an anguished day or two, she managed to overcome her qualms, and stayed where she was.

She was a beautiful girl, with blue eyes and her head a cluster of dark curls; she had an expression of great sweetness and gentleness. Everyone who knew her liked her, till the time of her death in 1967. She sang as she worked, in a kind of low contented croon. She was not otherwise musical, but perhaps the half-destroyed music of Celtic bards, and the work-chants, lived on in her. There had been great poets once in her part of the Highlands: Mackays too.

It is likely that my parents met at a local dance or social. (Permission to go to dances occasionally had to be wrung from the hotel proprietor, by the chambermaids and waitresses. Those underlings went so far as to threaten strike action. Their hours of work were long and hard, by present-day standards.)

At first she did not like my father very much. She thought him too forward and familiar, especially when he kissed her unexpectedly the first time they were together. But that kiss kindled a marriage that lasted for thirty years, till my father died in 1940.

They were married in Strathy in June 1910. A company of tinkers came past and danced at the wedding. The mailship *St Ola* was dressed in flags for their voyage back home. My father was popular enough for that honour to be paid to him and his bride. He was thirty-four at that time. My mother was nineteen.

✧ ✧ ✧

Children came at fairly regular intervals – my sister Ruby in 1911, Hugh in 1913, John in 1915, a brother Harold who died in infancy in 1917, Richard (Norrie) in 1919, and myself in 1921.

Early years are remembered in gleams only, and the gleams illumine what seem to be quite unimportant incidents. I remember sitting up in my pram, aged maybe two or three, and watching the silhouette of my father, in his postman's hat, against the window; he seemed to be reading a sheet of paper. But why that simple image remains, while thousands of other images lie buried forever in the unconscious, is a mystery.

Another early memory is of sitting on the doorstep when a tinker woman came to the door selling pins and haberdashery. As a child I was so upset by people and events that were not part of the everyday life of Stromness, that I fainted where I sat. A dream remains from childhood: I am sitting in a tinkers' pony-drawn cart, and we are going on a country road. I have never had a dream so vivid. They are taking me far away, up and down little hills.

Another memory is of the crew of an Aberdeen trawler; they are all drunk and staggering on the street. Whether I really saw this, or whether some neighbour woman told it at our open door, I can't now remember; but the image of those dangerous strangers on our quiet street filled me with dread.

A few years later, on a New Year's Day, I saw two of our local fishermen staggering on the street. They were both of them peaceable familiar men; the sight of them behaving in this bizarre way sent me hurrying home, white in the face. Later, one of my mother's friends said, 'May the fear of drink stay with him for a long time.'

I mention those trivial events because later, when I first began to write, tinkers and drinkers entered frequently into my stories and poems – too frequently, for many readers.

One reason, I think, is that such people are possessed of a wild precarious freedom denied to most people who are on the diurnal treadmill of money-making and accepted behaviour and whose days are folded grayly together. Actually, I have learned that this is not so; the life of everyone is unique and mysterious. Under all the accumulations of custom, boredom and drift lies somewhere 'the immortal diamond' spoken of by Gerard Manley Hopkins. Edwin Muir would have called it the 'Eden', a pure racial inheritance going right back to the Creation. I have often been intrigued by a latent snobbery that very many people, even the poorest and wretchedest, keep hidden somewhere about them; at the faintest encouragement they will tell you, in a secret proud whisper, how in fact they are not what they seem, they stem from an ancient proud lineage, they are connected with some duke a couple of centuries back, or going further into the mists, with a famous Viking jarl. I have wondered at the comfort such memories, of very doubtful validity, bring to ordinary people. It may be a spoiled fragment of the Eden that is such a wonderful symbol in Muir's poetry, or a distorted whisper of the intimations of immortality that Wordsworth had. I wonder at this preoccupation with the broken fragments of lost kingdoms myself – this gazing into stones as if they were jewels – because I have never had the least desire to know for sure that I'm descended from an earl or a great hero. I remember whispers in our house, in childhood, that somehow we could trace a descent from King Hakon, the tragic hero of Largs; but that must have been childish romancings of my sister and brothers. My father would have stamped sternly on such idle dreams: kings and millionaires meant nothing to him – his heart was always with the very poor and the dispossessed.

Twentieth-century literature has taken up the theme of the ordinary ineffectual man: Joyce's Leopold Bloom, Eliot's Prufrock, Beckett's Estragon and Vladimir, Mann's Hans Castorp, Chekhov's drifters and dreamers on the edge of social catastrophe. It is remarkable that in modern literature it is the common man who holds the rarest treasures. There, lost, is the 'immortal diamond'.

The first house I remember was in a sea-close just off the main street of Stromness. There, on the pier, fishermen worked at their lines and lobster-creels. The townsfolk went their ways on the street above. The little town was full of shops in the 1920s, some of them sweetie-shops kept by old women. These were places of delight. I took my Saturday half-penny to one or other of them. One part of my childhood seems to have been a continuous ache for sweet things. Items of food we were told were nourishing and good for us, like porridge, broth, mince, stew, fish, I had to be wheedled into tasting. Apple puddings were quite another thing, and the sponge-cakes and little biscuits and buns my mother baked every weekend, and pancakes hot from the griddle.

At last it was time to go to school, at the age of five. The school was an immense forbidding building, more like a prison, at the back of the town, half-way up Brinkie's Brae.

My mother remembered how I came home from school after the first morning, threw my little satchel into a corner, and said, 'I'm never going back there again!' But to school I was dragged or cajoled every morning until in the end I was broken in.

Compulsory education was only half a century old when I went to school. Looking back on my schooldays, I have the feeling that the whole educational system in Scotland must have been hurriedly cobbled together by some committee of pedants; and Scotland has always been full of learned puritanical humourless men. There was nothing amiss with the primary aim, which was to teach all children 'the three Rs' – reading, writing, arithmetic. These skills most of us achieved after a few years. But afterwards it was like a great mill grinding out sterile knowledge; there was no room for delight or wonderment. We were made to understand soon enough that life is real, life is earnest.

After the mastering of 'the three Rs', I still shudder when I recall how English was taught. The language was a corpse, and we were little apple-cheeked apprentices of

28

post mortem. A sentence would be taken from some text –
the duller the better – and we spent long periods applying
'parsing' and 'analysis' to this piece of dead meat. I still
cannot understand how parsing and analysis ever helped
one of us to enjoy the bounty and richness of the language.
On the contrary, to many children that cutting up and
examining of parts must have given to literature and language a charnel-house revulsion. I am thankful that it did
not have this effect on me. I think I must have uncon-
sciously rebelled. At any rate, I never mastered the intricacies of English as a machine, or as a museum of
specimens. To this day I can't parse a simple sentence, and
could only manage to analyse a more complex sentence
with a mighty furrowing of brows, and maybe then not
entirely correctly . . I hope that parsing and analysis have
been long abandoned in Scottish schools.

Nor was there delight in the verse and prose we had to
read. Spelling was driven into us at the rate of ten or twelve
words a day, and if we had gotten more than three wrong
after our homework we were beaten with a leather strap on
the palm of the hand. Every week we had to learn by heart
a verse or stanza of poetry. There was no joy in that, either:
it was another groan and grind of the wearisome mill-
wheel.

But fragments of the verse did find lodgement in some
niche of the spirit somewhere, to be remembered later with
delight:

> There sometimes doth a leaping fish
> Send through the tarn a lonely cheer;

The crags repeat the raven's croak,
In symphony austere;
Hither the rainbow comes – the cloud –
And mists that spread the flying shroud;
And sunbeams; and the sounding blast,
That, if it could, would hurry past;
But that enormous barrier holds it fast.*

And the mournful cadences of *The Burial of Sir John Moore at Corunna* were never forgotten.

Geography seemed to be lists of the capitals of countries, and rivers and mountain ranges, and the main imports and exports. There was a huge map of the world on the classroom wall, liberally splashed with red. We soon got to know that those red patches comprised the British Empire, and that we were a part of it; and I know that our little hearts beat proudly because of it.

History: that was a list of the Kings of Scotland from the early medieval Kenneth MacAlpine, and the battles they fought, and the turbulent nobility they had to control. There was one great period in the fourteenth century, the War of Independence against England. That was magnificent! That was thrilling beyond words! The dreariness of school was almost compensated for by the great victories of Wallace and King Robert the Bruce against the massed chivalry of England, culminating in the famous victory of Bannockburn in 1314.

The tragedies of Flodden and Mary Queen of Scots gave

* William Wordsworth, 'Fidelity'.

me – and I'm sure other ten-year-olds too – a lump in the throat.

Eventually, in 1603, it was the King of Scotland who became the King of England too – and Great Britain came into existence, a political entity that over the centuries went from strength to strength, nearly always victorious over the French, the Spanish, the Danes – and the first little red splashes began to appear here and there on the map of the world.

True, there were setbacks. The American colonies were ungrateful enough to renounce allegiance. Napoleon gave us a series of shocks until he was broken at Waterloo.

Internally, there were thrilling episodes like the Civil War and the trial and execution of that serene stubborn monarch, Charles I. And the marvellous tragic attempt of his great-grandson Prince Charles Edward Stuart to oust the German usurpers of the throne.

History was the only subject in school that made the blood sing along my veins, but it was the romantic spindrift of history, not the great surges of tribes and economics and ideas that are the stuff of history. But I am grateful for what we got; it nourished the imagination.

I think that those who framed Scottish education in the late nineteenth century were driven by a sentiment that has been a constant in Scottish thought: that one is put on this earth to 'get on', to 'better oneself'. Though the Scots have always claimed to be the most democratic of peoples, a curious snobbery has always been there, certainly since the Industrial Revolution. According to this ideal, the lowest kinds of labour are those of the land and the inshore waters. Crofters and fishermen, who were so important in Orkney society (being the majority), were held to be at the bottom of the pyramid. I never recall this as being overtly told us, but it was always implied. The duller pupils left school aged fourteen; if they could get employment in a grocer shop or a draper shop, they had done well; they were on a level almost with apprentices to a trade. At least they would never have to filthy their hands with clay or fish-slime. A few became sailors and that was only a small step up, unless they went on to become ships' officers or master mariners, and then their life was an undoubted success. Many young men from all the Scottish islands made distinguished careers for themselves at sea.

A step higher than shop assistants or craft apprentices was to get work as a clerk in a lawyer's office or a bank.

The supreme achievement of Scottish pupils was to obtain the Higher Leaving Certificate. This was the key to college and university. If you went to Edinburgh University – it was the university favoured by Orcadian students before the Second World War – and became a doctor, a minister, a teacher, or a lawyer, you had justified your existence, nothing better was to be hoped for. Many Orkneymen, a whole cluster of them, have become professors (chiefly in scientific disciplines) all over the world. The blend of Scandinavian and Scot has produced such vintage minds.

Even my father, who was a democrat, subscribed in a way to this Smilesian philosophy; always, however, with reservations. He would say to us children, again and again, 'Whatever happens, keep humble' . . . 'Never get

above yourselves'. Do I imagine it, that he recited Bunyan
to us?

> He that is down need fear no fall,
> He that is low, no pride.
> He that is humble ever shall
> Have God to be his guide.

Whether he actually quoted us this or not, it was his life-
long philosophy. But there was sufficient Scottishness in
him to tell us about the poor croft boy that he remembered
going to school barefoot, and with a peat under his arm to
keep the classroom fire burning. This boy became eventually Dr John Gunn, a director of Nelson the publishers,
editor of the famous *Orkney Book* of 1909, and the author
of several stories for boys.

I mention those things because when I came to write in
the 1950s, I drew much of my inspiration (if such a thing
exists) from the tillers of earth and sea that the whole
engine of education had been devised to lift the worthy
ones and the hard studiers clear of. I came, as the years
passed, to see the farmers and fishing-folk, and their work,
as the most important in any community. Where would
they be, the generals, the poets, the law-givers and the
philosophers, without their primal labour? It seems to me
that the best people I have known, the richest and the truest
characters, were farmers, fishermen, and sailors. Beyond
them, free on the outer fringes of society, drift the wandering ones and the hard drinkers: necessary symbols. But
without the workers on land and sea I think I would not

have written a story or a poem. I often wonder what I
would have become, if I had been brought up in a large city
like Glasgow or Birmingham. All I am certain about is that
my writing would have had a different, thinner quality, if it
existed at all.

The educational system made grudging curtsies in the
direction of the arts. What was forced on us children was
dreadful beyond words. The once a week music period
seemed to consist almost wholly of 'ear-tests'; the teacher
struck a sequence of notes on a piano and we were supposed to write down what we thought she had played, in
sol-fa, in our notebooks. (I never had the least idea.) By
way of relief, we sang traditional songs. For many years,
the very word 'music' roused a distaste in me.

Art: the teacher would set a jug on the table, and we had
to draw it in pencil, shading it and putting in 'the high-
lights'. At this skill I was one of the worst in the class.
Sometimes, by way of variation, a duster would be draped
over the jug – it was thought, I suppose, that the folds of
the duster would sharpen any skill we had. No appeal was
ever made to the imagination, except that perhaps near
Christmas we would be told to design a Christmas card.

So, the free joyous spirit of childhood was penned and
confined; and, in some cases no doubt, crippled.

But the argument of the Olympians in Edinburgh would
have been: 'What's the *use* of art or music or poetry? Will
that help them when they go at last to serve at counter or
office desk? – even less, if they return to the ploughland or
fishing boats. To the successful ones – the professionals –
the arts will serve, maybe, to fill a passing hour.'

So utterly stupid was the system that one or two periods were set aside each week for what was called 'drill' (physical education). Being children born into the boundless freedom of the elements – immense sea and sky and shoreline, and hills where we could wander freely at weekends and all the long summer – we had the fluency and grace of young animals. What 'drill' was supposed to do for us I cannot for the life of me conceive; but it consisted of long lines of boys being ordered to contort their bodies into rhythmic jerks and spasms, over and over again, like puppets. A young lady teacher in a gym tunic presided over this nonsense.

Our true energy we kept for football, swimming, boating, and for those mysterious games that children have played in Scotland for centuries perhaps: 'pikka', 'leave-o', 'rounders'.

The girls played skipping games with primitive chants; often with beautiful words to them, but edged with mockery and melancholy.

❖ ❖ ❖

There was a weekly class called 'composition', which consisted of the writing of little essays. I suppose it must have been conceived with the object of making us adequate in the use of English, for even crofters would have to write two or three letters in the course of their lives. Extraordinary subjects were given us to write about: 'A Day in the Life of a Gamekeeper' or 'The Life Story of a

Tree', or 'How I Spent my Summer Holiday'. Composition was a subject dreaded by most of the pupils. To me, writing came effortlessly, while all around my classmates grunted and sweated to get a few more words out. I really couldn't understand it when week after week our teacher said, 'George Brown has written the best composition again' . . . And one week she said, 'He can write so well because he reads good books.'

But in fact I had no taste for 'good books' at all. What we boys devoured were the magazines published weekly by D. C. Thomson of Dundee: *Adventure*, *Wizard*, *Rover*, *Hotspur*, *Skipper*. They cost twopence each. We were too poor to buy them all; a good deal of swopping and exchanging went on. For some reason which I can't even now explain to myself, it was the English public-school serial stories that appealed most strongly to me. Two magazines called *Gem* and *Magnet* contained only public school stories – one was about a fat greedy cowardly mendacious boy called Billy Bunter, and his schoolmates who were forever tormenting him; Billy was a kind of simple degenerate Falstaff. 'Oh,' I would think to myself, delighting in those stories, 'if only my father was a rich man and could send me to a public school!' It seems now from the many first-hand accounts we have of life in those English public schools that for sensitive boys they were places of utmost misery, with only a gleam here and there, now and again; and that in fact the Orkney school we went to, bad though it was, was a place of sweetness and light in comparison. I think what attracted many of us boys was that life in those posh schools seemed to consist of fun and practical jokes, endless 'tuck-boxes' and mysterious games like cricket and rugby, with minimal studying. I remember weeping over a sentimental novel of public school life called *St Winifred's, or, The World of School*, by Dean Farrar, in which a pious much-bullied boy melts into a Dickensian death, like a snowflake into light. There was another tear-compelling school novel, *The Fifth Form at St Dominic's* . . . Not Shakespeare nor Tolstoy nor Thomas Mann have succeeded in drawing a single tear down this iron cheek.

I think I have wasted too much space on Scottish education in the 1920s and 30s. It tried casting us into a mould, and partially succeeded. For a boy who was to become a writer, it was a nuisance and a waste of time at best. I am grateful to it for the three Rs; it is possible that had I been born in 1821 rather than 1921, I would have been barely literate. On the other hand, I have a strong feeling that there is no such creature as a 'mute inglorious Milton' . . . A person with innate talents will bring them into use, somehow or other, sooner or later – nothing on earth will stop him but death itself – for he is the talent and the talent is him, inseparable.

The poets who composed the great Border ballads were probably illiterate. Perhaps much of the strength of those ballads comes from the fact that they could not read or write. The art of writing literature makes marvellous leaping fountains among the formal gardens and the statuary, from cunningly contrived conduits and pumps; but the early epics and ballads are from the pure strong rock of the spring itself, that is somehow akin to the blood in our veins and to the ebbings and floods of the sea.

When I was a boy I was always intrigued by the name 'Anon' at the end of some poems in our verse-books. Anonymous, I was told – the name of the poet is lost. Again I have the feeling that not one man made those great ballads; in a real sense they are the work of an entire tribe or community. One illiterate man might indeed have rough-hewn them with his voice; thereafter, being vividly uttered and remembered, they are part of the inheritance of a community. Words and phrases, and whole quatrains, are changed over generations to conform to the life of this market-village or that hillside farming community. The wandering minstrels are abroad – a few of them poets too – and now and then a crude phrase gets touched to felicity or purest magic. Time flows over the ballads, and wears them to this shape and that. Such ballads as *Lord Randal*, which has variations even inside Scotland, were carried across the Atlantic and now have American accents and images. One phrase of Thomas Mann struck me, that art is somehow 'anonymous and communal'. Over the past four centuries there has been too much emphasis on the life and personality of authors – great streams of reminiscence, biography and autobiography. In fact the lives of writers are not greatly different from the lives of plumbers; except that, in the romantic age, writers struck poses and behaved in wild eccentric ways – not so much because those aberrations were a part of their nature as because the public expected it of them: 'true genius is to madness near allied'. In the late nineteenth century no poet or artist was genuine unless he broke most of the social rules, steeped himself in drink and laudanum, got syphilis or consumption, fled to wild barren places of the earth, manned barricades, was alternately in a trough or on a crest of the spirit, flirted with the demonic or the angelic (or both). It seems to me that under all the masks, the lives of artists are as boring and also as uniquely fascinating as any or every other life. They put their name and copyright to every novel, poem, sonata, or painting; but in fact the works are not theirs only but have come from the whole community in which they live. Tolstoy understood this, and acted on it.

School continued to be a prison-house when we passed from primary to secondary education. There we were taught Latin, algebra, geometry, physics, chemistry, French. At the very end of five or six years of higher education, I – and some of my contemporaries too – began to sense a meaning in what we were doing. The hated Latin class began to yield treasures – Caesar's war commentaries, Livy's history, haunting lines from Virgil – '*Sunt lacrymae rerum et mentem mortalia tangunt . . .*'. I always felt myself to be an alien in the school science laboratory, though the teacher there, a Kirkwall man called John Shearer, was the kindest and ablest teacher I have known; he was such an extraordinarily good man that he seemed to be particularly kind to the backward ones in his class, like me.

Even the once-hated mathematics began to intrigue me, here and there. I glimpsed, now and then, the lovely forms and strict necessities of geometry; a pleasure akin to music, I realised later.

Shakespeare was hurled at our heads at the age of

twelve: *The Merchant of Venice*. I think a few pupils were
bruised and stunned: twelve-year-olds are too young to be
fed on Shakespeare. Yet the first line of Shakespeare that I
experienced intrigued me: 'In sooth, I know not why I am
so sad/It wearies me . . .'. Those words should be carved
over the lintel of my door: in a way they express perfectly
my life and my way of looking at things – a tremulous
melancholy, a mystery through which are glimpsed and
guessed from time to time forms of beauty and delight.
Sometimes it has seemed to me that 'Thy will be done' is
the only prayer worth uttering, because it comprehends
everything.

By the end of *The Merchant of Venice*, a few of us in that
class were enchanted by Shakespeare. It was a joy, not a
burden, to have to stand up and recite Shylock's great
speech, 'Signor Antonio, many a time and oft . . .' and
Portia's 'The quality of mercy . . .'. We went on to read, in
the years following, with increasing delight, *A Midsummer
Night's Dream, Julius Caesar, Henry the Fifth, Twelfth
Night, Hamlet, Macbeth, Lear*.

✧ ✧ ✧

But my imagination had been quickened much earlier, in
childhood. My sister was ten years older than me; when I
was about five or six she told me stories, usually romantic
stories of unrequited love. *Willie Drowned in Yarrow*: the
image lingered of a straw hat floating in the water, where
Willie had drowned going to the love tryst. But she had a

whole quiver-full of stories, in many of which the heroine 'died of a broken heart'. It seemed a good enough way to round off a story.

Death is only a word to a child, unless someone in his own family is cancelled. I heard, wonderingly, that my grandfather in the Highlands had died. Once my mother and brother Norrie and I had spent a holiday in the little croft at Braal, Strathy. To me the bearded old man seemed stern and austere. He read out of a Gaelic Bible and prayed aloud in Gaelic every day. Once, when all the heads were bowed and the eyes closed, I slipped away from the circle of worshippers, out onto the moor. There was trouble about that when I got back at last. And once I fell in the river, and came back sodden and wretched. Strathy seemed to me to be a desolate place, very different from the little corn-patched hills of Orkney. My grandmother was a kind sweet-natured woman. She would give me a cup of warm milk at the byre door. At Thurso, going home, my mother took my brother and me to see a train, thinking we would be much impressed. 'I've seen better-looking trains than that,' said I, 'in books . . .'. Yet from that Highland desolation I get my gift of poetry, perhaps.

✧ ✧ ✧

Literature entered the mind stealthily, like a thief; only it was a good thief, like Robin Hood or Brecht's Asdak, and left treasures instead of taking them. One or two periods a week in the primary school were devoted to religious education. Miss Smith, our kind sorely-tried teacher, read us stories out of the Old Testament. To me, they seem still to be among the greatest stories ever told: Abraham and Isaac and Jacob – how hairy Esau was cheated of the blessing – how Joseph the dreamer was set upon by his brothers and sold into Egypt, and the blood-stained coat of many colours was brought home to the grieving father; and the amazing transactions that went on in the fullness of time between Pharaoh's chief minister and the wandering desert tribe. All this was rich food for the imagination.

Somehow there came into our house a copy of Grimms' *Fairy Tales*. I read story after story with the greatest delight. A year or two later I got hold of Andersen's *Fairy Tales* but there was no magic in them for me. They may be too subtle for the mind of a young child.

About the age of fifteen, the fogs dispersed, and I found myself on that peak in Darien. The poetry of Shelley and Keats was pure intoxication. It was the words and the sound they made, not the essence, that enchanted me. Perhaps it was Shelley's 'To a Skylark' that set me off, then *Adonais*, 'Ozymandias', 'Ode to the West Wind', 'Music when soft voices die', some choruses from *Prometheus Unbound*. Shelley's younger contemporary Keats was even headier stuff, especially 'Ode to a Nightingale'. I heard, with wonder, that he had written it in one morning sitting in his Hampstead garden. His death at the age of twenty-five was shocking, and yet there was a kind of wonder about it, and also about Shelley's sea-change at the age of twenty-nine. Many of Wordsworth's poems seemed beautiful too – 'Earth hath not anything to show more fair', and the Lucy lyrics, and such lines as 'Breaking the silence of the seas/Among the farthest Hebrides . . .'. The lives of those romantic poets were almost as fascinating as their poetry – I learned with distaste that Wordsworth had lived on to the age of eighty, and become more and more reactionary the older he got. At this time I was an ardent revolutionary, like Shelley. The word 'socialism' had not come into the language in Shelley's lifetime; but I was a Shelleyan socialist.

Not all poetry gave me this feeling of tipsiness. The arch-romantic, Byron, left me cold, except for a line here and there: 'She walks in beauty, like the night/Of cloudless climes and starry skies . . .' and 'The Assyrian came down like a wolf on the fold/And his cohorts were gleaming in purple and gold'. I think, in part, it was his sneering references to Keats, the marvellous boy, that put me off Byron: 'Strange that the mind, that very fiery particle/Should let itself be snuffed out by an article'. Except for some passages here and there in 'L'Allegro' and 'Il Penseroso', I had a distaste for Milton, both the man and the poet. 'Lycidas' struck me as a rough-hewn uncouth poem: it was only years later, when I had matured, that the marvels of that elegy revealed themselves, veil after purple veil.

The same may also be said of Shelley and Keats. The words were an immediate intoxication. Ten or twelve years later, bit by bit, the poems began to yield their full richness; and now, in my late middle age I find, still, another facet from the hoard will gleam out suddenly.

It seems to me now that the 'Ode on a Grecian Urn' is a much better poem than 'Ode to a Nightingale'; but in my teens I hadn't liked its austere pure contemplation. In 'Nightingale', one reels from wineshop to wineshop.

The verse of the eighteenth century seemed a huge desert – Dryden, Pope, Thomson. Again, it was only in my maturity that their marvellously polished couplets made sense. But Goldsmith's *Deserted Village* made an immediate impact.

Burns couldn't be avoided, because Burns, especially towards the end of January each year, was on everybody's tongue: mostly it was the sentimental Burns of 'Bonny Mary of Argyll', and 'The Cotter's Saturday Night' vintage. The powerful rollicking poetry – 'Tam o'Shanter', 'Holy Willie's Prayer', 'Death and Dr Hornbook', 'The Jolly Beggars' – kept its treasures until I was ready to appreciate them. But 'To a Mouse', which we had to learn by heart, made an immediate appeal, though many of the Scottish words were strange to us half-Nordic islanders.

I thought it wonderful that there were poets writing now, today: for surely the mighty harvests had been reaped, and we were living in the age of the *Wizard*, the *Daily Express*, and the *Christian Herald*. But no: some lyrics were given us to learn by heart – Masefield's 'Cargoes', and 'I must go down to the sea again . . .' and Yeats' 'Lake Isle of Innisfree' – and they were very enjoyable. I got hold of an anthology with some T. S. Eliot in it; 'Rhapsody on a Winter Night' seemed like a piece of imbecility. Only when I was in my early twenties did Eliot begin to chant his litanies.

As for prose: every week in class we had to read three chapters from a Scott novel, so that we could answer questions about it on the Friday afternoon. Something similar happened, I'm sure, in every Scottish secondary school. The official attitude was, 'Scott *must* be read, for he is a "classic", and close acquaintance with him will improve the mind, and give it tone and resonance . . .'. The effect of this kind of forced reading on me was to give me such a distaste for Scott that even today I can't open one of his novels with any pleasure. I have read *The Pirate* thrice, at different periods of my life, hoping that age would make me wise to its merits. Each time I closed the book with relief. I don't know of any of my contemporaries who has any relish for Scott, and yet the man enchanted the whole of Europe with his novels when they were first published. Of all that hoard and squander, there remains only a lyric or two, 'Proud Maisie is in the wood' and 'Look not thou on beauty's charming'. We were dosed with R. L. Stevenson too, and John Buchan, with (for me) the same result; though many of my contemporaries were spell-bound by *Treasure Island* and *Kidnapped*.

It was by stealth that I came on books and stories that meant something to me: one tale (I forget the title)* by Conrad, about two seedy characters in charge of a river trading post somewhere in Africa; and *The House with the Green Shutters*.

I stayed on at school till I was eighteen, content to drift from classroom to classroom. I had no vocation for any trade or profession.

---

* Probably 'Heart of Darkness'.

Every boy and girl goes through the stage called puberty, before they emerge as adults, eager for what is to come.

I was not eager for what was to come. I shrank from it; I dreaded it. I don't propose to dwell on the two or three years of my life, between the ages of fourteen to sixteen probably, but they were wretched years, full of shames and fears and miseries. What made that time so particularly dreadful was that there was no one I could unburden myself to. Outside the classroom, pupils and teachers had nothing to say to each other. My parents had too many worries to have time for the nameless terrors of their youngest son. I don't know if my contemporaries were enduring those things too; but I remember sitting in the classroom like a youth shunned and branded. It was agony for me to have to speak in class. It seemed that I sat there for weeks and months with my hand covering my face. It actually happened that way. I wanted no one to notice me.

If I was to describe my state of mind at this time, it might be of interest to a psychologist, but the common reader would scarcely be interested. I will just say that I yearned back towards my childhood, and dreaded what was to come. One symptom was that whenever my mother left the house to go shopping, I was convinced every time that she would never come home again. I would shadow her along the street, and dodge into doorways if she chanced to look back. I can't remember how long this state of affairs went on, but it's certain that a part of my mind was unhinged.

All this while I was smoking cigarettes, whenever I could lay my hands on twopence to buy five Woodbines, the cheapest brand on the market. I was completely dependent on them – and I was a dedicated smoker, drawing the smoke deep into my lungs. (I had begun to smoke about the age of twelve.)

Round about the same time, a particularly severe epidemic of measles went through the school. I emerged from it very much shaken physically. The disease damaged my eyes and ears; fortunately, after a year of semi-deafness, my hearing returned. But my sight was never as good as it had been. Worst of all was the weakness in my lungs, and that, I know now, was compounded by cigarette smoking. I ought to have known that something serious ailed me, because in my early teens I had been as wild a boy as any of my contemporaries; we all went free as birds between the hills and the piers. I was particularly good at football, and I revelled in it. The game had a special magic for us; the young local men who formed the team Stromness Athletic were heroes to us schoolboys. If they defeated one or other of the Kirkwall teams – which they frequently did in the early 1930s – we boys were in a heaven of delight. In those days only the better-off houses had a battery wireless set. What joy, on a Saturday afternoon, to sit in some 'rich' boy's house and listen to a football commentary from Glasgow or Edinburgh or Aberdeen, when the great Scottish clubs were embattled; though the reception was far from good, prickly with crackles and the volume sinking and swelling like waves of the sea. The cities of Scotland were as far away as the moon. I never entertained a hope of ever visiting one, or seeing an actual game. But I had a favourite football team – Glasgow Celtic – and one of the most awesome days of my childhood was when news came that the Celtic goalkeeper, John Thomson, had died going down to save a certain goal. On that occasion Celtic had been playing against Rangers, their arch enemies. The death of John Thomson affected me more, I think, than the fate of Mary, Queen of Scots, or the defeats of Flodden and Culloden, that I had grieved over in my history book. A religious element came into the Celtic–Rangers rivalry, for Celtic was predominantly a Catholic team, and Rangers absolutely Protestant, so that even today no Catholic player or official is on their books. Why I chose Celtic to support I do not know; but there is a mysterious element in it somewhere.

In later life I was drawn to the Catholic church, and a few years ago I wrote an essay for *The Tablet* about my conversion. The following, based on *The Tablet* article, tells all there is to say.

The sermon was the kernel of the Presbyterian services on which I was brought up. The old folk considered that for a minister to read his sermon was a blemish on him. The prayers, too, had to be impromptu. The choir, organ, and congregation joined in the singing of psalms and hymns. Some of those metrical psalms have magnificent tunes, and some of the translations are fine poetry:

> Now Israel may say,
> And that truly,
> If that the Lord
> Had not our cause maintained

If that the Lord
Had not our right sustained
When cruel men
Against us furiously
Rose up in wrath
To make of us their prey . . .

We knew little about Catholicism. There were no
Catholics in the little town I was brought up in, except an
Italian ice-cream seller and an Irish barber. There was a
Catholic church and priest and a small flock in Kirkwall,
fifteen miles away. The chief splendour of that town is the
Cathedral of St Magnus the Martyr; years were to pass
before I knew that the red minster had been built by
Catholics in the twelfth century for Catholic worship. At
the Reformation there was none of the violence and
burning in Orkney that afflicted Catholic shrines in other
parts of Scotland; St Magnus' Cathedral sailed intact
through the tempest. The Orcadians had never been
'enthusiasts' in religion; and I never heard Catholics
denounced or reviled; still, there was something sinister in
the very word Catholic; all the words that clustered about
it – rosary, pope, confession, relics, purgatory, monks,
penance – had the same sinister connotations. I can't
remember that we were ever instructed to hate Catholicism
or Catholics; it was just that Catholicism and its mysteries
lay outside our pale, and it was better so. We Presbyterians,
so it was implied, were enlightened by comparison, and had
travelled on, far beyond medieval idolatry and superstition.
  Scotsmen being great hair-splitters in matters of philo-

sophy and religion, there were three Presbyterian churches in our little town – plus the Episcopal Church, the Salvation army, the Pentecostals, and the Plymouth Brethren. I suppose the few of us who thought about the plethora at all wondered why it should be so. Why were the followers of Christ so divided?

Purgatory, if ever I thought about it, seemed a reasonable and acceptable state. For where was the person in our society so good that he or she was ripe for heaven immediately – or where, on the fringes, was there a layabout or a no-good that didn't have some gleam of humour and kindness in him? The ore would be none the worse for a purifying.

Our English master one day read to the class Francis Thompson's 'Hound of Heaven'. I think, looking back after forty-five years, that the poem has many flaws in its pure gem-like flame; but I could not have enough of that wonderful discovery. I read it over and over, until I had it by heart. And I knew that the man reeling from delight to vain earthly delight was a Catholic – a very sad and weak and fallible one – and that the Hound in relentless pursuit of him was Christ, or the Church. And, for some reason, these facts gave to the poem an extra relish.

When I was in my mid teens I read Lytton Strachey's *Eminent Victorians*, which contains his famous essay on Cardinal Manning, who, it was soon apparent, the author disliked very much. John Henry Newman was, for Strachey, the perfect counter-balance. He had more than a passing sympathy with Newman, as a true child of the Romantic movement who wrote moreover an exact and luminous prose; but Newman, too, of course, had been fatally lured and fascinated by the enormous claims of Rome, that apostolic succession that went back eighteen and a half centuries to St Peter. And then Strachey demonstrates gleefully how the dogmas and utterances of one pope were contradicted out of the mouth of another pope. What could any average rational being make of such a morass of error and human frailty and pretension?

And yet the whole pageant that Strachey unfolded before me – intended to make every reader chuckle scornfully – gave me one of the great thrills I have got out of literature.

That such an institution as the Church of Rome – with all its human faults – had lasted for nearly two thousand years, while parties and factions and kingdoms had had their day and withered, seemed to me to be utterly wonderful. Some mysterious power seemed to be preserving it against the assaults and erosions of time.

The phrase in some book that finally, for Newman, led from Anglicanism to Catholicism (implying that this or that theological tenet was true, because the pope of the time had said it) made me catch my breath, and not in derision either, as Strachey had intended. It was the same kind of astonishment as Newman had felt; though much diluted of course.

Soon I got hold of Newman's *Apologia*, most of which (the personalities and feuds of Oxford in his day) bored me, except for those passages, all exquisite and soaring as violin music, that rise clear above his own dilemmas and difficulties.

I read many books about this time, including accounts of

conversion to Catholicism, but none remains in my mind except for the bizarre and melancholy tale of Frederick Rolfe, Baron Corvo.

I read the history of Orkney in Viking times, *Orkneyinga Saga*, an anthology of deeds of heroism and vaunt and 'derring-do'; out of the waste-land of fire and revenge, the story of the martyrdom of Earl Magnus shines like a precious stone:

So glad was the worthy Earl Magnus as though he were bidden to a feast . . . He prayed that God's angels would come to meet his soul and bear it into the repose of Paradise . . . After that he signed himself with the cross, and bowed himself to the stroke . . . That spot before mossy and stony, but a little after there sprung up a green sward where he was slain . . . There had then passed since the birth of Christ one thousand and ninety and one winters.

The Orcadians, if they thought about Magnus Erlendson, considered him to be a queer fish, one of those medieval figures, clustered about with mortifications and miracles, that have no real place in our enlightened progressive society. For me, Magnus was at once a solid convincing flesh-and-blood man, from whom pure spirit flashed from time to time – and never more brightly than at the hour of his death by an axe-stroke, in Egilsay island on Easter Monday, 1117.

Was this Magnus a Catholic or not? In western Europe in the twelfth century there were only Catholics. And the

Cathedral in Kirkwall had been built by Catholic masons, for the offering of the Catholic Mass.

It seemed a thing of the utmost simplicity and wonderment to me.

Yet no Scotsman takes precipitate action. I lingered for years in this state of acknowledging Catholicism, while doing nothing about it. In the Scottish town of Dalkeith near where I was studying in 1951/2, I went to mass twice or thrice, and was disappointed – I got lost in the Missal, among the long silences and the whispers; and the hymns and the worshippers with their beads were strange to me. The devotion of the working-class women did move me: here they found beauty and peace in the midst of drab lives.

Yet I felt that, in spite of all, here was the Church that had been founded on the Rock.

And still I delayed, for another ten years.

In the end it was literature that broke down my last defences. There are many ways of entering a fold; it was the beauty of words that opened the door to me:

> Love bade me welcome; yet my soul drew back,
>   Guilty of dust and sin . . .*

The beauty of Christ's parables was irresistible. How could they fail to be, when so many of them concern ploughing and seedtime and harvest, and his listeners were most of them fishermen? I live in a group of islands that

* George Herbert, *The Temple: Love.*

have been farmed for many centuries; all round me in summer are the whispering cornfields turning from green to gold. 'Except a seed fall into the ground, and die . . .'. Those words were a delight and a revelation, when I first understood them. And at piers and moorings in every village and island are the fishing boats, and the daily venturers into the perilous west, the horizon-eyed salt-tongued fishermen ('The kingdom is like a net . . .'; 'I will make you fishers of men . . .'). The elements of earth and sea, that we thought so dull and ordinary, held a bounteousness and a mystery not of this world. Now I looked with another eye at those providers of our bread and fish; and when I came at last to work as a writer, it was those heroic and primeval occupations that provided the richest imagery, the most exciting symbolism.

That the toil of the earthworker should become, in the Mass, Corpus Christi, was a wonder beyond words, and still is. That one of the Pope's titles is The Fisherman, an acknowledgement of his descent from Simon Peter the fisherman, was an added delight to the mind and spirit, and still is.

'You must sit down,' says Love, 'and taste My meat.'
So I did sit and eat.*

The mystery and the beauty increased, as I read more widely. Graham Greene's *The Power and the Glory* impressed me deeply; for here was a hunted and driven

* Ibid.

54

priest, and in many ways a worthless one, who nevertheless kept faith to the end, as better martyrs had done in other places.

From every age and airt of literature poems and prose swarmed in to increase the beauty and the mystery I had wandered into, it seemed by accident, so long ago. If 'beauty is truth, truth beauty', here were beauty and truth beyond price. A few fragments of such truth and beauty, like treasures long lost, were sufficient; the way of argument and reason were not for me.

When thou from hence away art past
(Every nicht and all)
To Purgatory fire thou comest at last
(And Christ receive thy saul).

If ever thou gavest meat and drink
The fire shall never mak thee shrink.

If meat and drink thou ne'er gav'st nane
The fire shall burn thee to the bare bane.*

*

Maiden and moder
Was never non but she
Well may such a ladye
Godes moder be.†

*

* Anon., 'The Lyke Wake Dirge'.
† Anon., medieval, 'I sing of a Maiden that is makeles'.

For the Islands I Sing

The corn was orient and immortal wheat . . .*

*

And I must enter again the round
Zion of the water-bead
And the synagogue of the ear of corn[†]

*

Within the cloistre blissful of thy sidis
Took manne's shape the eternal Love and Pees[‡]

*

La sue voluntade è nostra pace[§]

*

Wherever a Catholic sun doth shine
There's always laughter and good red wine[**]

*

I want . . .
a black boy to announce to the gold-minded whites
the arrival of the reign of the ear of corn[††]

*

---

* Thomas Traherne, *Centuries of Meditation*.
† Dylan Thomas, 'A Refusal to Mourn'.
‡ Chaucer, 'The Second Nonnes Tale', *The Canterbury Tales*.
§ Dante, *Paradiso*.
** Hilaire Belloc, 'Wherever a Catholic'.
†† F. García Lorca, 'Ode to Walt Whitman'.

For the Islands I Sing

Thou mastering me,
God! giver of breath and bread;
World's strand, sway of the sea;
Lord of living and dead . . .*

In principio erat verbum. Can it be that those beauties of literature and all the arts are a striving to return to that immaculate beginning? – the word lost in The Word.

✧ ✧ ✧

To return to football. Within a very short time I lost all my skill and enthusiasm. I didn't know it at the time, but already the 'tubercle bacillus' was in me, not raging but burning with a slow smoulder for which the old name, consumption, is a good description. Going up the steep lane to school, I had to stop to get my breath. And I began to cough up thick phlegm.

The mind is a complex labyrinth. When the medical officer confirmed that I had pulmonary tuberculosis, 'an open lesion at the apex of the left lung', I was horrified. In 1941 there was no cure. One simply lay in a sanatorium bed and hoped for the best, with the help of fresh air and wholesome food. There was a kind of treatment that had worked in some cases: gold injections. For months this increasingly dense fluid with solid grains held in suspension was injected into the muscle of the upper arm – a

* Gerard Manley Hopkins, 'The Wreck of the *Deutschland*'.

painful business. At the end of the course of treatment I was neither better nor worse. I stayed for six months in the little sanatorium, set high on a brae above Kirkwall.

In some ways I was actually grateful for the tubercle. It saved me from the world of 'getting and spending' that I had dreaded so much. If there was to be much of a future at all, it would be passed in a kind of limbo where little or nothing was expected of me. By this time the dreads of adolescence had faded. I was not so ill that life was a burden, I could eat and sleep and laugh with the nurses and patients. Vaguely I turned the pages of books. I had *The Golden Treasury* on my locker: I remember what delight Swinburne's 'The Garden of Proserpine' was. In some strange way I even exulted that I had been branded with the same illness as Keats, Stevenson, Emily Brontë, Francis Thompson, D. H. Lawrence.

My father had died suddenly in 1940, soon after the defeat of France. One of the last things I remember him saying was, 'Thank God the boys won't have to go to France.' His four sons were of military age. My father's generation remembered the frightful carnage on the Western Front in the 1914–18 war.

As soon as this new war broke out, thousands of soldiers poured into Orkney to protect the naval base of Scapa Flow. It is reckoned that at the height of the war there were 60,000 troops encamped in ugly little Nissen-hut villages all round the perimeter of Scapa. German bombers flew in from Norway; our ears got attuned to the undulating drone of their engines. Then in the falling darkness searchlights probed and criss-crossed about the sky, anti-aircraft shells burst in puffs and clusters (that some old women took to be German parachutes descending); and the islands shook with Wagnerian noise. After the summer of 1941 the air raids ceased; Hitler needed all his bombers for the Russian front.

The morning of the invasion of Russia I remember going into the little ward of the sanatorium where a padre lay listening to the news on headphones. He was, I think, a Congregational minister, and had been on his way to Iceland to minister to the troops when he had a lung haemorrhage. The troop-ship had put in at the nearest port, Kirkwall, and there the Revd Collins-Williams lay, slowly recovering. 'Whom the gods wish to destroy, they first make mad,' he said to me, referring of course to Hitler.

In October the little English doctor, who was probably a kindly man though he had an intimidating way with him (and the slow-spoken Orcadians could never attune their minds to his loud hectoring voice), said I could go home. 'But you're not cured,' he said. I knew that the slow smouldering was going on and on in my lungs. The danger was that the smouldering might break into a flame, in which case there was little hope; it would be 'early dark'. I think, at the time, I had little fear of death; I may even have been half in love with it, like Keats.

Time stretched ahead, for whatever length, a desert, with here and there a little oasis of poetry. I was unemployed and unemployable. Of course they would not have me in the services. I had no money. Like Bernard Shaw, I threw my mother into the battle of life. But that's too energetic an image; she would have seen to it that I never starved. With only mild occasional murmurs of complaint, she kept me in food and cigarettes and clothes. The situation was eased two years later, when a small weekly allowance was paid by the government to tuberculosis sufferers. I gave my mother £1 a week, and kept ten shillings to myself; and I felt as rich and free as a lord.

In this desert of time, I began to write poems. None of them, fortunately, survives. One was a sonnet about sea-gulls, and a line remains in my mind: 'the seagulls traverse long corridors of intense sound . . .'. There was a Latin teacher at the school who had written poetry and had had his verse published in magazines. He was conservative in his tastes – he could see no virtues in T. S. Eliot or Ezra Pound or Auden. But in the Georgian tradition he had written some beautiful lyrics. Occasionally I would send Mr Cook – who had taught us to like Virgil and Ovid – a sheaf of my verses, and he criticised them in a constructive way, though he objected to the 'new influences'. (By this time I was beginning to be fascinated by Eliot and Auden and Spender.) Once John Cook said, 'I think you'll be famous by the time you're forty.' But when I was forty I was still a very shadowy figure in literature.

I never dared to hope that one day my poems would be published in a book. I remember that John Cook typed one or two of my poems; to see them in typescript sent a tremble of joy through me. The writing of them was a hobby, a pastime, a foible. I enjoyed 'the making'. The tubercle still smouldered inside me. Against the day when the flames broke out, I made those little word-constructions perhaps. One well-known Scottish poet, William

Soutar, who died about this time (1943) after years of illness, had written a line, 'Gang doon wi' a sang, gang doon . . .'.

There were so many servicemen in Orkney between 1939 and 1945 that households were encouraged to take in soldiers as lodgers. Among the soldiers who stayed at our house was a captain in the Education Corps, Francis Scarfe. I was thrilled to learn that Francis Scarfe had published two books of poems, and was a regular contributor to *Poetry London* and *The Listener*. He had published a critical study of modern poetry called *Auden and After*. Before his calling-up, he had been a lecturer in French literature at Glasgow University. He was in his early thirties, and an agreeable man. In the evenings we would both sit at the table writing verse, gravely passing the finished poems to each other, for comment and criticism. Francis Scarfe enriched part of a year for me. He was full of enthusiasm for Eliot, Lawrence, Dylan Thomas. He must have encouraged me to persevere with my writing. But after a time he was posted elsewhere outside the islands. For forty years, we wrote to each other at Christmas. He died in 1988, in Oxford.

Another kind office Francis Scarfe did for me was to introduce me to classical music. One day he brought home from the large wooden hut that housed the offices and library of the Army Education Corps a small wind-up gramophone and an album containing Mendelssohn's Violin Concerto in the heavy 78 r.p.m. discs. My ears brimmed with enchantment! There followed 'Eine Kleine Nachtmusik', a Mozart horn concerto, Schubert's Fifth

Symphony, Beethoven's Eighth and Ninth symphonies. The great outpouring of joy in the choral movement bewildered and excited me – such an affirmation, it may be, strengthened my spirit to opt for life, at a time when 'easeful death' seemed the more likely way.

I began to write articles, news items, and book reviews for a local newspaper, the *Orkney Herald*. I had too much imagination to be a good correspondent; occasionally it got me into trouble. C.P. Scott of the *Manchester Guardian* had made the famous remark, 'Facts are sacred, comment is free'. I tended to take the opposite stance, 'Facts are free, comment is sacred'. (Poetry is always at war with journalism.)

In Shetland – the group of islands to the north-east of Orkney – a monthly magazine was published, *The New Shetlander*. I began to send poems and stories to the editor, Peter Jamieson. Actually to see my words in print put April in my spirit. (But when, fairly recently, I stumbled on some of my work *The New Shetlander* had published, I blanched with shame.) The eventual distaste I have for nearly everything I have published persists. Even as I write this I feel the inhibition, *it's not what it should be*.

I tried my hand at a little play, set in the Viking period. I remember that finishing it gave me a small but agreeable surge of power. Walking along the street the next day, I felt for the first time like a free townsman: no need to slink from doorway to doorway like a leper any more. I had made something that I knew in my bones to be good. I showed the play to a few friends, who were impressed. I went so far as to send it to the well-known Orkney novelist, Eric Linklater, in a wretched-looking typescript (for now I had an old typewriter). He sent it back with a few kind constructive words. It was a piece of gross impertinence on my part. Nowadays, I am often sent poems and other bits of writing by beginners. Only now and then – but rarely, very rarely – is there any discernible promise. My heart sinks when another sheaf of apprentice poems falls from the envelope on to my table, and I feel irritated. Then I remember the scruffy typescript I sent to Eric Linklater, and I grow more considerate. And sometimes the heart does quicken at some felicity, some well-turned stanza. There *might* be a new poet drawing breath in this harsh world.

That old play, written in 1942, has returned to the dust.

The stories, poems, plays were coming now in a steady stream. Sometimes the radio would broadcast a short piece of mine in a magazine programme. All these little achievements gave me a feeling of confidence, and might even have infused a kind of strength into me. At any rate, my illness got no worse.

I had known for some time that there were other Orcadian writers. I have mentioned Eric Linklater; his early novels, set partly in Orkney, gave me great delight: *Whitemaa's Saga, Magnus Merriman, The Men of Ness*.

I read the autobiography of Edwin Muir, *The Story and the Fable*. He grew up in the small fertile island of Wyre, on his father's farm. The early chapter of that book, about his childhood, is a very beautiful piece of writing, and reminds one again and again of the accounts of infancy written by Vaughan and Traherne, Wordsworth and Dylan Thomas ('Fern Hill'). Occasionally a poem by Edwin Muir would appear in *The Listener*; I found them, in spite of a visionary light, difficult. Edwin Muir is one of those poets to whose 'realm of gold' a key must be found. In 1946 his book of poems *The Voyage* appeared. The key had been in my hand all the time – I read *The Voyage* with delight.

I got to know, too, that Orkney possessed a medieval literature, *Orkneyinga Saga*. Here was another realm of gold. The desert was actually becoming interesting: the oases lay thicker around than I had imagined, and nearer home. If, in my late teens, I had had the death wish – and so intensely that it destroyed a part of my lungs, I think – now life might be worth living after all. The smoulder inside me was almost quenched.

I fed deeply on those stories out of *Orkneyinga Saga*. Besides being magnificent stories in themselves – the rivalry between Earl Thorfinn and Earl Rognvald the First; the feud between Earl Hakon and Earl Magnus; the pilgrimage of Earl Rognvald the Second to Jerusalem, Byzantium, Rome; the extraordinary career of the Viking farmer, Sweyn Asleifson, who every winter sat at his fire in Langskaill, Gairsay, with eighty retainers – they are told by a genius. Whoever he was, what he set down was 'pure narrative', from which everything that might interrupt the flow of the story (description, comment, reflection) is excluded. The characters reveal themselves in a few curt words. A murder or a sea-battle is inset with verse – not the kind of poetry you or I are used to, but short intricate webs of alliteration and kennings. Everywhere there are flashes of humour. One quickly realises that those early Orcadians had a horror of old age and slow witherings: better to die young in a siege or sea-battle; best of all to die with a jest in your mouth that men will remember for generations.

I don't know if Hemingway read the sagas; of modern story-tellers he comes closest to the spirit of them: though some readers have detected, under Hemingway's bravado, a kind of inverse sentimentality.

I think that, in the writing of narrative, I learned a great deal from *Burnt Njal, Grettir, Orkneyinga Saga*. It is good, for certain kinds of writing, to use as few words as possible. The structure and form of the saga stories are magnificent. I think I have learned from them the importance of pure shape. But from my mother's side, the Celtic, I delight too in decoration. Look at the intricacies of early Gaelic art. Whether it is desirable to marry 'pure narrative' with elaborate decoration is not for me to say. I write as I must.

Only a few books, only a few authors, alas, make one feel the way Keats did when he first opened Chapman's Homer.

I can never forget my first reading of Forster's *A Passage to India*. (I must have read it ten or twelve times, since.) One afternoon, in the Stromness bookshop, I took from the shelf the Everyman edition of *Selected Stories* by Thomas Mann. I think I must have bought it because there was nothing else to read, on that particular day. The Ancient Mariner's hand fell on my shoulder. I sent for *The Magic Mountain*; it gave me days of intense delight. There is no doubt that writers whom one enjoys so much are taken into the creative imagination and influence one's writing; though one should never be so foolish as to imitate them.

Much later, I was writing a long play called *A Spell for Green Corn*. I was having great difficulty with at least one of the scenes. That play caused me much pain and sweat. The poet Iain Crichton Smith loaned me a book of Brecht's plays. *The Caucasian Chalk Circle* entranced me from the first page. Seeing how Brecht had shaped that masterpiece, I saw at once how the 'impossible' part of *A Spell for Green Corn* must be shaped. My pen hovered and sang like a bird over the manuscript for a few days.

❖ ❖ ❖

I mentioned earlier that Stromness was a 'dry' town. There had been too many drink-tempests in its history, when the nineteenth-century whaling men came home at the end of summer, when Irish labourers and English marines clashed at closing times, during the First World War. How strongly Stromnessians were drawn to alcohol appears in the *New Statistical Account* of 1842, where the Revd Peter Learmonth records that nearly forty drinking shops, inns, ale-houses existed. A strong reaction set in; an ardent eloquent Temperance Movement was active; after the 1914–18 war Stromness voted itself dry. So I grew up in a prohibition town. I only saw drink in our house round about New Year. I remember furtive groups of men, on the last day of the year, waiting for the Kirkwall bus to bring their festive whisky.

But in 1947 the situation was reversed. Stromness voted itself 'wet'. Six months later the main hotel opened two bars and there was a licensed grocer.

I went in, drank a glass or two of weak beer, and was immediately 'hooked'. I remember how, in the months following, we used to approach the bar door furtively, looking to right and left, covering the last few yards quickly. It was still a shameful thing to be seen entering a 'den of iniquity'. But in time I grew a carapace.

Scottish pubs in those days were bare spartan ugly places, as if even the publicans acquiesced in the questionableness of this kind of enjoyment. (There were, it's true, cocktail bars, with modish furnishings and plants, and dim lighting, for the professional classes and ladies – but she was a bold woman who darkened the doors of even the cocktail bar in Stromness for the first year or two – and the drink was always a few pence dearer there than in the public bar where the fishermen and the sailors and the farmers drank.)

The first few glasses of beer were a revelation; they flushed my veins with happiness; they washed away all cares and shyness and worries. I remember thinking to myself, 'If I could have two pints of beer every afternoon, life would be a great happiness . . .'. It was a comical bizarre slightly surrealistic world to which I had found the key. Over the years it has brought me happiness, laughter, and misery of mind and body. Apart from the anodyne of the drink, I found myself among a company of 'characters', as they are called in Scotland, a kind of chorus of men, whose comments on the passing scene and reminiscences were an abiding joy.

Sober, waiting for the bar to open, they were apt to be stolid and silent. Drink unlocked their tongues and made poets of them (though the only real verse they knew were the ballads of Robert Service and fragments of Burns). I delighted in their company. I learned, over the months that followed, that two pints of draught in the afternoon weren't enough to ensure permanent felicity. The favourite working-class drink in Scotland then, and perhaps now, was 'a half and a half' – that is, a small measure of whisky ('a nip') and a half-pint of beer. I soon discovered that whisky was a quicker way than beer to the realms of fantasy. Fortunately whisky was expensive, and I could afford it only occasionally. But if you have a sufficient quantity of 'halfs and halfs' under your belt, you can soon become drunk. I was frequently drunk; I earned a certain gray reputation in the town for over-indulgence. Sometimes I would be led home and left on the doorstep, or dumped inside like a sack of potatoes. On one occasion the police van picked me up, but either the one local cell was full or the officers were kindly disposed, because they drove me home. Next morning the neighbours whispered, 'George Brown was taken home last night in the "Black Maria" . . .'. This whisper, when it reached my mother's ear, incensed her (in so far as a woman of her serene nature could be incensed): 'They'll say anything but their prayers. It wasn't the "Black Maria" – I saw it myself – it was a *gray van* . . .' Her attitude to my over-drinking was a mild disapproval or a silent anger. Many an afternoon my dinner spoiled in the oven while I caroused and chanted in 'the chorus of Hamnavoe men'.

Sometimes, when I was hard up or mildly hung over, I

would stay in bed and write a poem or a story or a piece of dialogue. And now, since the opening of the pub, a new element entered my writing: the change, both good and bad, that alcohol puts on people. It gave me a kind of insight into the workings of the mind: how under the drab surface complexities, there exists a ritualistically simple world of joy and anger. It is well known that people who live in northern latitudes are much more given to drunkenness than the Spaniards or the Italians, where wine has always been an accepted part of life, and a blessing among other blessings. In the north it is considered shameful to show one's feelings and emotions. The stoical mask must always be worn, whatever befalls. But in alcohol – especially the fiery waters of whisky, aquavit, vodka – under the mask they give vent to their feelings, and because their emotions have been so closely pent up, tipsiness tends to have a carnival extravagance.

The writer in me seized eagerly on this Jekyll-and-Hyde aspect of the northern psyche. Literature delights in contrast. There are no drunks in Jane Austen; a good writer can detect subtle shades and contrasts by the turn of a head, the movement of a hand, or a few casual words. My coarser art has to make do with a man or a woman sober or in various states of drunkenness. The complexity of an 'ordinary person' is amazing – in northern lands, drink is the key – inside are treasures and rags-and-bones all jumbled together.

When my first book of stories, *A Calendar of Love*, came out in 1967, my mother said, 'It's all about drinking.' When I thought about it, what she had said was true.

I was hooked on drink for thirty years or more. But I never became an alcoholic, mainly because my guts quickly staled. I might get drunk for a day or two, more or less continuously, with intervals for sleep; at the end of the bout my stomach said, 'No more'. Time and again it called a halt, a thing for which I am grateful. With robust intestines, I might have become a full-blown alcoholic. But the mind too protested. Not only was it plunged into the miseries and depressions of hangover, but it insisted, 'Such a waste of time and energy! There's work to be done . . .' For a long time there was a divided allegiance, drink and writing. In the end, writing got the upper hand, but it continued to use the insights that drink had won for me.

At least once, about the dangerous time of New Year, I have been on the verge of delirium tremens. It was a foul experience. There is a state of drunkenness where even sleep leaves the wreck of the body. All one night I lay in bed open-eyed. I had to force myself to keep my eyes open, for whenever I closed them a sequence of evil depraved faces filed slowly through my brain; each paused as if to note my wretchedness, and passed on; and another hellish face took its place. It was like a sequence of photographs thrown on a screen: all portraits of the utmost frightfulness, hundreds of them. My only relief was to force open my eyes. But my body was so weary that when I lost concentration the eyelids fell, and another file of dreadful faces came in strict order.

Another New Year's night, I seized the books from the little bookcase at the stair-head and hurled them down, till they lay like shot birds in the lobby below. Finally I fell over my feet and tumbled helter-skelter down the fourteen stairs to join the books. My mother picked me up and put me to bed. She must have been hurt and worried, but there was something so bizarre in the discovery of her writing son in a dishevelled nest of books that she laughed wonderingly, telling me about it next morning. (There must be some deep psychological reason for this casting-down of the books.) I rose to drink again, and felt little pain, for Hogmanay is a festival of whisky bottles, and drink is an anaesthetic. Next morning, when I got out of bed, it was as if a red-hot knife had been plunged into my side. To laugh, to cough, even to turn, brought another wild stab. (So Caesar must have felt in his last moments at the Capitol.) The doctor, summoned, remarked that it was lucky for me that I hadn't broken my neck but only a rib. In a few days I was able to stand among the chorus of drinkers at the Pier-head, waiting for the pub doors to open at eleven o'clock.

Once, a few years later, I was arrested for being 'drunk and incapable' in Hanover Street, Edinburgh, and spent a wretched day in a police cell with two other drunks who turned out to be very pleasant men. We were, all three, in the miseries of withdrawal; yet what I remember about that day was laughter. One cell-mate was a sailor who had damaged his hand in a fight in a respectable Edinburgh coffee-house; I had to roll his cigarettes for him. The other drunk was an Englishman who happened to be in Edinburgh on holiday: he was mildly indignant because we didn't get a cup of tea. From time to time an elderly police-man came in and threw coal on the fire but, though appealed to, he brought no teapot or cups. The long day passed, in wretchedness and laughter. Late at night the cell door opened and a ragged dirty little man was pushed in. He kept shouting, 'I'll tell you this, I hate Catholics!' At last the sailor with the hurt hand remarked mildly that he was a Catholic. Then the Englishman who had longed all day for a cup of tea said that *he* was a Catholic. And I announced that I too was a Catholic. (None of the three of us had known this before.) At once the ragged little drunk beat on the cell door with his fists and kept shouting 'Let me out! Let me out! They're all Catholics in here! They'll kill me! . . .' Eventually he was taken away to another cell. I think the laughter that broke from us then more than out-weighed the degradations of the day.

Late at night I was released on bail of £3.

I never saw my cell-mates again, whom I had liked so much. Next morning I had to appear before the magistrate, along with the previous day's haul of drunks and prosti-tutes. The little ragged anti-papist was tried before me. He demanded in a loud voice to be X-rayed. When my turn came, I was admonished.

I have written so much about drink because it occupies an important part of my life and writing. Nowadays the thirst has largely left me – I could live without alcohol and never miss it. But I still drink from time to time, alone and among friends. 'And yet I know, where'er I go/That there hath passed away a glory from the earth . . .'. But it was a tarnished and a tainted glory, that brought me a good deal of anguish.

✧ ✧ ✧ ✧

I wrote from time to time, in the decade after the sanatorium, mainly poems, but without urgency, sitting up in bed between breakfast time and lunch. My mother would bring me breakfast upstairs on a tray – tea and toast and an egg: a ritual that I'm sure caused many a one to say, 'That lazy brute! All he does is drink and sleep half the day. That poor mother of his! . . .'

But I'm sure my mother was glad to have the house to herself, going about her tasks singing a tuneless happy song. As for me, I was writing my small poems, and reading books.

Since 1934 we had been in a new ugly council house on the outskirts of Stromness. Before that we had lived in Melvin Place, in an old dark insanitary house. This 'new house', in a block of four houses, with other blocks here and there in a field called Well Park, was thought by my mother and other members of the family to be great luxury, because it had a bathroom and gas lamps and a little flower garden in front and a vegetable patch at the back. My father died in 1940. Gradually the older children drifted away and got married. In the end only my mother and I lived there. The four neighbour women were always visiting each other. There was a little tea ceremony, every morning, in this house or that, round about eleven o'clock. My mother always read the tea leaves, but it seemed to me

73

she had only a few stock phrases – 'A tall dark stranger is coming to visit you . . .' 'There are three letters on the way . . .' 'You'll have a pleasant surprise at the end of the week . . .'. But the tea and the fortune-telling went on every day for years.

The council scheme was called Well Park because there was a well capped by a roof at one side of the field. Now it was foetid and dark, for every house in Stromness had running water. Eventually it was covered in. A little burn flowed past the well. After the winter rains the stream was a rushing gurgling torrent, white-flecked. I remember the happiness of summer mornings, waking up to hear corncrakes in the oatfield across the road, where there was a steep farm called Guardhouse. The corncrakes were silenced at last, like the well and the burn; for more ugly blocks were built in that field. The insanitary charm of the old town was gradually, over the decades, girt around by those functional blocks of houses that fitted so badly into the landscape. Later municipal architects showed more imagination. The old houses from the eighteenth century, instead of being demolished, as had happened until fairly recently, kept their original shells and façades, while being thoroughly renovated inside.

Outside the chorus of drinkers, I made other friends: Ian MacInnes who came to teach art at Stromness Academy in 1949, and his wife Jean, and their eldest daughter Sheena to whom I told bedtime stories; Gerry Meyer who came from London to be editor of *The Orcadian*, and his Stromness-born wife Nora. I visited their houses often, for talk and laughter.

One day in the bookshop in Kirkwall, Leonard's, the assistant approached me. His name was Ernest Marwick and he was a farmer's son from the parish of Evie. He told me that he was compiling an anthology of Orkney verse; he wondered if I wrote verse, and if so, would I let him see some manuscripts? He seemed to be quite impressed by the sheaf I posted to him. It wasn't long before I got to know Ernest Marwick's circle of friends. The most notable of them was a small dark man, very deaf, with great whorls of eyebrow. His name was Robert Rendall. He was a local draper in his late forties, a bachelor, an authority on shells, and a theologian of that strict Evangelical sect called Plymouth Brethren. He was also a poet, and was about to publish locally a small collection of his poems to be called *Country Sonnets*. He was working on a long study of the sonnet-form in Scotland.

Robert Rendall was an extraordinary man, whose stillness would be shaken from time to time with sudden enthusiasms – an image for a poem; some new idea for the classification of shells based on the mathematics of their whorls; an impulse to visit Birsay or Italy. Once the seed had taken root in his mind, there was no rest for him until it was accomplished. And he must tell everyone who might be at all interested, at once. Janette Marwick, Ernest's wife, used to tell me how Robert Rendall would call at Westermill (the Marwicks' house) half a dozen times a day, brimming over with enthusiasm. He would laugh like a boy at this new idea he had stumbled on, in high shrill glee. His almost complete deafness seemed to be no handicap to him then. One day in the 1950s, he came thrice to my hospital ward to report on the latest felicity in a sonnet he was wrestling with. His last visit was in the evening. The work was finished. He was flushed with achievement. He recited to me one of the most perfect sonnets I know: 'Renewal'. Robert Rendall published four small books of verse. Among them are ten or a dozen marvellous lyrics, in the Orkney dialect – and so almost unknown outside the islands as yet. No future anthology of Scottish poetry dare ignore these perfectly-wrought pieces. Some of them are translations from *The Greek Anthology*.

The masterpieces in Robert's four books are companioned by mediocre poems too much influenced by the Georgian poets, especially Bridges, whom Robert considered to be a great master and innovator of prosody. Like John Cook, he had a distaste for T. S. Eliot and 'the Faber poets' in Eliot's fold. But, because Edwin Muir was an Orkneyman, he gave Muir's poetry serious consideration, and got to like much of it; so that, here and there in his own verse, there is an echo or a tone of Muir.

Other Kirkwall friends of Ernest Marwick I got to know – John Mooney the historian and his daughter Embla; his neighbours the Misses Costie, one of whom wrote good dialect verse; John Mackay, the Sanday headmaster, whose eyes seemed to glimmer perpetually with mingled intelligence and humour. Ernest's wife Janette was one of the gentlest and kindest women I have known. She belonged to the island of Sanday, and had been a nurse in Palestine and elsewhere. She was a devout Anglican, but there was no solemnity in her religion; her laughter was wholesome and good.

In strict contrast to my Stromness chorus of drinking friends, those Kirkwall scholars and poets and their acquaintances were Temperance folk. They knew for sure of my splurges and sprees, but our friendship remained true. I spent many happy weekends, or longer periods, at Westermill.

Ernest Marwick's *Anthology of Orkney Verse* came out in 1949. It is no provincial hotch-potch. Apart from the thousand years of poetry he selected from, it is a scholarly compilation, with lucid commentary and notes. Perhaps among the moderns he stumbled a bit; certainly I blush whenever my eye lights on the three immature mawkish poems of mine that are included.

But for indifferent health from his childhood on, Ernest Marwick would certainly have gone on to distinguish himself academically. He was as brilliant a man as any in that galaxy of Orkney professors of the preceding generation. History, folk-lore, literature: he had toiled and harvested in those fields. In his upstairs study in Westermill he would sometimes open his granary to me: folder after folder of carefully researched and lucidly expounded knowledge, entirely original. 'There's enough here for a dozen books,' I would say to him. But he was an anxious perfectionist. In the 1940s he published in *The Orcadian*, week after week, chapters of a social history of Orkney in the nineteenth century – fascinating material, brilliantly expounded. His intention had been to make a book of those articles, eventually. There were one or two breaths of criticism. Ernest was so deeply hurt that the book remains unpublished to this day. Again, towards the end of his life, Ernest was writing an autobiography.* Every life is unique. I am sure that Ernest's story would have cast a marvellous light not only on himself but on the society of farmers and crofters he grew up among – a book perhaps to rival Edwin Muir's *The Story and The Fable*. There were negotiations for its publication outside Orkney, by a famous publishing house. Eventually Ernest vetoed it. It remains in the great pile of manuscripts he left. Future generations of Orkneymen will have the benefit of his patient original research in – there must be – half a dozen books at least.

This gentle good man died suddenly one fine summer afternoon in 1977. The car he was driving left the straight country road and crashed into a farm steading in the parish of Rendall. All Orkney grieved for his death.

Janette Marwick lived for a few more years and died in Kirkwall. They were childless.

❖ ❖ ❖

In a way – on the surface – the years between 1941 and 1951 were years that the locusts ate. I drew my National Assistance money every week and spent most of it on beer and tobacco – by this time I was smoking a pipe – and on Penguin books. All the work I did was to write a few fugi-

---

* The autobiography remains unpublished. However, the following works by Marwick have been published: *An Anthology of Orkney Verse* (1949); *The Folklore of Orkney and Shetland* (1975); *An Orkney Anthology*, Vol. 1 (1991). Volume 2 of *The Orkney Anthology* has yet to be published.

tive pieces every week for the *Orkney Herald*. I never lit the
fire or made my bed or planted potatoes. My mother did
everything. Sometimes, if she went away for a few days, I
could boil an egg or fry a kipper, while the tidy house
slowly grew a shambles about me. It must have seemed to
the Stromnessians that I was a layabout, a ne'er-do-weel,
one of the kind who inhabit the fringes of every community. I was quite content with this role.

One of the great experiences of most lives never happened to me – I never fell in love with anybody, and no
woman ever fell in love with me. I used to wonder about
this gap in my experience, but it never unduly worried me.
There were girls that I thought pretty and attractive and
sweet; but in their presence I was immediately awkward
and withdrawn and put on a frown. I had no homosexual
urges, apart from one, when I admired another slightly
older schoolboy in my class, and for a while couldn't have
enough of his company and his talk. I would seek him out
by devious ways. To meet him on the street suddenly was a
magical thing: I was shaken with sweet secret delight. This
infatuation lasted for part of one summer, then broke like
a bubble; and he who had been the adored hero went about
in the light of common day again. Many adolescent boys,
I think, have this experience. It never happened to me
again.

Yet, in that decade, I had certain very intense experiences
that became part of the fabric of my life. I did not will them
and I did not go in search of them. I am often chided nowadays for my passivity – why don't I go to beautiful places;
why don't I travel to Norway or Iceland even, whose cul-

tures have influenced me so much? Surely a writer must always be hungry for all that life can offer – the world is there to be plundered, the way D. H. Lawrence and Somerset Maugham and Graham Greene went, saw, experienced, enjoyed, and put all at last into books. I don't have an answer. Travelling even the short distances I have gone bores me, and I am continuously (while the journey lasts) apprehensive. I think, in a spasm of panic, I must be on the wrong train, going through the night towards Newcastle instead of Perth. I have to be reassured by my neighbour in the compartment, sometimes more than once.

Some kind of ancient wisdom whispers always, 'Stay where you are. What is good and necessary for you will be brought or you will be led to it. Wait. Have patience. What has been written down for you will happen when the time comes.'

What we desire and what we strive for rarely happens, or the outcome is quite different from what we intended, or expected. T. S. Eliot expresses it perfectly:

What you thought you came for
Is only a shell, a husk of meaning,
From which the purpose breaks only when it is fulfilled,
If at all . . .*

Most of those intense experiences have come from literature – *A Passage to India*, *The Magic Mountain*, *The Caucasian Chalk Circle*, *Orkneyinga Saga*, the Border

---

* T. S. Eliot, 'Little Gidding'.

ballads – which seemed to touch a core and change every-thing – 'renewed, transfigured in another pattern'.

While I was a patient in the sanatorium in 1941, after a while I was let out to wander like a cloud. I drifted one day, inevitably, but for the first time, into St Magnus' Cathedral in Kirkwall. Except that the experience was intense, I can't remember the details, apart from the one thought, 'I would like to be buried in this place.' (No one will ever be buried there again.) The cathedral and the reason for its building, and the building of it, and all that happened in it, have quickened my imagination again and again. Of late years, in the south-east corner of the Cathedral, there has grown a cluster of plaques to Orkney's writers and scholars. I would be glad, I suppose, to have my name and years there, after my death.*

✧ ✧ ✧

One Sunday afternoon, in the summer of 1946, I was invited to be one of a picnic party to the island of Hoy. (During the war it had been difficult to move among the islands: only troops and the shifting of them here and there was important.) Hoy is quite different from the other Orkney islands, which are in the main low and fluent and green, except for Mainland and Rousay that have modest hills only. The hills of Hoy (which means 'high

---

* The Island Council's Cathedral Committee have agreed to have this done.

island' in the old Norse) rise up stark and blue and sudden from the kirk and school and post-office and crofts at their base. The face of the Ward, the highest hill, is scarred and forbidding. Its neighbour, the Coolags, is a line of hills ending in magnificent cliffs that front the Atlantic. Eric Linklater has a good image for the Coolags: a lion couchant. The rock stack, The Old Man of Hoy, stands in the West with its feet in the ocean. Between the Ward and the Coolags winds the old Rackwick road, that now is eroded like a dried-up river bed: it is like the Psalmist's valley-of-the-shadow. At the end of this road is a sea valley called Rackwick: a green bowl gently tilted between the hills and the ocean. That Sunday, the beauty of Rackwick struck me like a blow. Once it had been a populous valley, but already it was drained of most of its people. Many of the little croft-houses were derelict; decay was beginning to eat into others – the roof flags were slipping, doors hung on rusty hinges. Slow fires of rust were devouring the pots inside and the iron ploughs at the gable-ends. It seemed a melancholy place, threatened with imminent utter desolation. I thought of Goldsmith's *Deserted Village* perhaps. I certainly thought of the island valley of Avilion 'where falls not rain or snow or any hail/Nor ever wind blows loudly'; because soon after I got home, with magic in my eyes, I wrote a prose-poem about a king who was carried to Rackwick for the cure of his battle-wounds. I thought it a good piece of writing at the time, but it is long dust and silence. A lasting spell was cast on me that Sunday, as we sat on the grass with our sandwiches and tea, and heard the slow boom of sea on stones and sand, and saw the two immense sea cliffs that guarded the valley.

I have returned to Rackwick many times since 1946. The symbol is lodged in many of my best stories and poems, and gives them any radiance and power they have.

It may be that art, looking before and after, exists to celebrate a good way of life that has vanished, and may be again. We must always be on our guard not to romanticise: life in a place like Rackwick must always have been stark and dangerous and uncomfortable (imagine three generations crammed into two small rooms, with little privacy, and the men with the salt dampness never out of their clothes, so that the torments of rheumatism and bronchitis came often with age). Yet I believe that their closeness to the elements, their pursuit of whale and herring and their anxious tending of the corn all summer, the winter flame on the hearth that their own hands had dug from the moor, while – if the harvest of sea and land had yielded an adequate bounty – the cupboard was well stocked till spring; that kind of life is more meaningful by far than the lives of people who set out each morning for an office by train with *The Times* to read; a holiday in Spain with wine and sun the only oasis in their desert.

Stanley Cursiter painted in Rackwick. Ian MacInnes owns a cottage, Noust, at the shore, and lives and paints there at all seasons of the year. Early in 1960 Sylvia Wishart visited Rackwick, and at once she too was touched with the enchantment. She hastened to rent a cottage, North-house, that was beginning to fall apart.

Once a hearth-fire is out, which has burned night and day, winter and summer, for generations, it is as if the heart of the house had stopped beating; decay sets in at once, rot and mildew begin their operations. I remember looking through the webbed window of North-house one summer day about 1960. I seem to remember a scattering of cups and plates and jars; table and box-bed and chairs; and even a picture askew on a wall (was it of Queen Victoria?). Sylvia Wishart decided to save North-house from time's ruin. The roof was thatched, cracks sealed, windows washed and brightened, stone floor scoured, and the heart of the house began to beat again (though the fire was coal in a stove, for the open hearth-fires were gone for good, along with the ancient skills of cooking and baking with pot and griddle hanging from hooks). There she lived often – and still does, from time to time – and painted many beautiful canvases of the hills and the sea. I got to know and like that cottage well. Rackwick is only a few miles from the shops and closes and piers of Stromness; but there the appetite has a special urge and edge, and there is more relish in food and sleep and work. Everything seems simple and clean.

Sylvia did a series of fine drawings for my book *An Orkney Tapestry* (1969).

To Sylvia Wishart

Salt in the wind, and corn.
Your green valley
Lies tilted to the shifting Atlantic gleam

For the Islands I Sing

Vacant now,
It waits, an overturned grain jar,
Abandoned in the world's flight from poverty, silence,
                                        sanctity.

When will people return again to Rackwick?
I see a thousand cities broken,
Science
Hounded like Cain through the marches of atom and
                                        planet,
And quiet people
Returning north with ox and net and plough.
They will offer it again to the light, a chalice.

In 1970, while I was staying with Archie and Elizabeth Bevan in another restored cottage at the shore, Mucklehouse, above the shallow sea cliff, a young man named Peter Maxwell Davies called. It was one of those miserable afternoons of cold drifting sea-haar, when even the lovely encircling hills of Rackwick look like a group of old hags keening. On such a day the spell touched the composer. The haar thickened into a cold rain. He set out with Archie and Elizabeth to find a cottage where he might live and work.

I wrote an impressionistic piece some years ago, about the day that Max Davies came to Rackwick:

Peter Maxwell Davies in Rackwick

The sea valley hugged by a cold gray haar, one Sunday in July.

Inside, on the range of Mucklehoose, a great pot of stew simmered.

A guest was expected: Kulgin Duval. He was in Stromness, on holiday from Falkland in Fife. He would spend the day with us, and return on the ferry to Stromness that evening.

He came, Kulgin: as always, with news. Kulgin never comes dully into a house. Since you saw him last, events and people have clustered about him. Events and people cluster about everybody, 'men and bits of paper'. Kulgin touches all people and happenings to an intensity akin to drama. Today he had something special to tell.

Kulgin, crossing on the ferry *Watchful*, from Stromness to Hoy, had met two young men, strangers. In those days (1970) hot coffee came free from the galley to passengers. Kulgin offered his flask of Highland Park whisky to top up their coffee, to the young men. One of them was carrying a book called *An Orkney Tapestry*. Kulgin said he knew the author – he was on his way to visit me (the author) and my friends, Archie and Elizabeth Bevan.

Kulgin arrived through the gray wet valley, loaded with sweets for six-years-old Anne Bevan.

Would we mind if a composer, Peter Maxwell Davies, and his agent, Jim Murdoch, called briefly later on?

At the moment composer and agent were being driven round Hoy in a hired car by Isaac Moar the Postmaster. Rackwick would be the end of the road.

Archie and Elizabeth are deeply interested in music. They wouldn't mind, they said. There was enough stew for all.

For the Islands I Sing

There were one or two scrapings of light in the sky. Sometimes, towards noon, a dull morning can break into green and blue and gold.

The guests arrived, among such half-promises.

They were immediately invited to stay for a meal.

The young dark composer – Beethoven in his twenties might have looked like him – told us he was looking for a house to compose in, as far away as possible from London.

The promise of fair weather didn't last. The thickening sea-fog obliterated the ghost of the sun. It hugged hills and sea. The haar condensed, spattering brigstones and windows with rain.

The valley – much restored since – was scattered with ruins of old abandoned crofts twenty-odd years ago. In such weather, the lyrical valley becomes ugly and shrunken; the hills, shawled in gray, seem like old eternal mourning presences.

No one could wish to live in such a morass, seeing it for the first time.

The composer was alert and interested. The ruined crofts were possible. They could be restored. Rackwick was the kind of place he was looking for.

Not even the good stew and the red wine could make me sanguine on such a day.

Archie suggested Burnmouth, a ruin nearest the beach, not so dilapidated as the others.

They set out, wrapped in coats and hats, for Burnmouth. The valley was lost in a gray wet cloud.

Kulgin and I sat at the table and drank from the jero-

87

boam of red home-made wine: beakers full of the warm south.

The house-hunters returned. The composer had liked what he saw of Burnmouth. One thing against it was that it lay on the path to the beach, and on summer days there might be too many tourists. What he wanted most was solitude.

Some other croft, maybe?

It was obvious he was impressed with Rackwick, even on such an atrocious day. Did he guess at the loveliness under the wrappings of rain and fog? The boom and hush and echo of the sea were everywhere.

What he could not have seen that day was the very highest croft in Rackwick; the haar had washed it from sight: Bunertoon, high up, at the end of the sheep path, across a deep watercourse, was lost there that day near the verge of the high cliff.

Max and Jim Murdoch and Kulgin went back to Stromness on the evening ferry.

I thought we might not see or hear word of the composer again.

But he wrote, near the end of winter, wondering if he could spend a few days after the New Year in Mucklehoose? The tenant, Dr Derrick Johnstone, readily gave his permission.

He returned in the dark of the year. He bought rubber boots and oilskin from John Wright's shop in Dundas Street. He bought meat and bread and cheese and a bottle of Cutty Sark whisky. We lunched in the Stromness Hotel. We were a bit late for Ginger Brown's ferry, and the ferryman gave us a sharp tongue-lash.

Midwinter in the north has its own intensities and clarities. It must have been then, in the cold diamond of the sun, or under the arch of winter stars, that he came on Bunertoon. The roof was off. The sheep had long had it for their own, a winter shelter.

Bunertoon – 'above the township' – was well restored a year or two later by David Nelson.

Between then and now, Max Davies has written, in Bunertoon, most of his music . . .

Now the valley, so imperilled, is stirring with new life. House after house has been restored. In summer it is full of people, and young rucksacked tourists come and go like birds or clouds. A few years ago the one remaining farmer, Jack Rendall, married and the first child to be born there for half a century opened her eyes on the storied light: Lucy. I wrote a little poem to celebrate her coming, and Max Davies clothed the words in music: and 'Lullaby for Lucy' was sung at the St Magnus Festival, by the cathedral choir.

> Let all plants and creatures of the valley now
> Unite,
> Calling a new
> Young one to join the celebration.
>
> Rowan and lamb and waters salt and sweet
> Entreat the
> New child to the brimming
> Dance of the valley,
> A pledge and a promise.

Lonely they were long, the creatures of Rackwick, till
Lucy came among them, all brightness and light.

I began in the 1960s to write poems about Rackwick.
When a cluster of poems about a single place gets thrown
quickly on to the page, the poet begins to discern a pattern,
and the pattern draws into itself more and more poems. In
1972 a whole poem-cycle on Rackwick was published,
called *Fishermen with Ploughs*. I think the book contains
some of my best poems. I mined far back in time, and
imagined the first-comers to the valley, a tribe that has left
a Norwegian fiord in a great ship because they are intoler-
ably threatened by 'the Dragon'. What the Dragon is I leave
to the imagination of the reader – the depredations of a
stronger neighbouring tribe, overpopulation and a short-
age of food, an utter necessity to break new horizons (for
it seems the westward drift of tribes is a constant in Indo-
European history: surge, settlement, then westward sun-
led seeking again after many generations). The middle
sections of the book take as their theme the life of the
Rackwick people through the centuries, until the people
drift away and one by one the houses fall into ruin. I think
I made a mistake in imagining, in the final section, a return
to Rackwick, but a branded and a brutish return, for a
nuclear attack has thrown a few ill-assorted people into a
ship, and a ruthless skipper guides them to the deserted
fields and scattered stones of Rackwick, for a new beginning. Again, I leave it to readers to work out if there is
indeed the germ of a new time or if those city people have
brought the last smoulderings of atomic fire with them,

and must inevitably perish. It is a chorus of the seven women of Rackwick who tell of those terrible hopes and fears. Women, perhaps, see deeper into the true heart of things than men, who busy themselves too much with externals and surfaces, and seem to be the only discoverers and heroes.

✧ ✧ ✧

In the winter of 1950/51, I joined an evening class out of boredom. One night after the class, the director of adult education, Alex Doloughan, asked me if I would consider becoming a student at Newbattle Abbey, Dalkeith. This adult education college had recently reopened after the war and the Orkney-born poet Edwin Muir had been appointed Warden. There would be a grant available – £150 – if I was accepted.

Edwin and Willa Muir were in Orkney that summer on holiday. They invited me to have tea with them in the Stromness Hotel. Edwin Muir said he had read a story of mine in *The New Shetlander*; on the strength of it he would take me as a student, beginning in October.

They were kind and reassuring. To embolden myself for the ordeal of the interview I had drunk a pint or two of heavy beer in the bar below. I needn't have feared. Edwin was kind and considerate, while Willa told robust and rollicking stories, laughing delightedly at the amazed look on my face. They had given a lift in their car to two fairground boxers, who had thanked Edwin for his kindness. 'And', said one boxer, 'we thank your mother too . . .'. She really did look older than Edwin, for arthritis had set its clamp on her limbs and shoulders.

At Newbattle, a small group of us students talked about books and writing day after day. It was a devoted group: Bill Drysdale would sit up half the night in the library writing a long play in the Shavian mode. Bob Fletcher from Airdrie wrote slowly and painfully: to write an essay took weeks of hard and concentrated work. He wrote one or two poems, as brief as Emily Dickinson's, but their birth was hard. Bob Fletcher was a dark heavy-moulded young man, direct and honest in his speech; the groundswell of his humour gathered far out and its onset was slow and ponderous, until it broke with joy or mockery, and left lingering echoes in library and crypt. There was a deep smouldering passion in him, for the things in life he held dear: 'the rights of man', and poetry. In literature his two great heroes were Milton and Herman Melville. I imagine that both those writers might have had a similar temperament to Bob; he saw his own moods and affections mirrored in their work. He never tired of quoting passages from *Paradise Lost* – and I would reply with the last great chorus of *Samson Agonistes* ('Come, come, no time for lamentation now . . .'). Melville's *Billy Budd* had him by the heart: the story of the handsome fated young sailor in the man-of-war haunted him with its pity and purity. Like Billy Budd, Bob faced up to the injustice and evil of life, seemingly baffled and tongue-tied; until he asserted truth and right, not like Billy Budd with a death-blow, but with a long slow considered thunder of language, that had passion and satire in it. I imagine him as being in descent from the best of the Scottish Calvinists, true austere somewhat intolerant men. Though our outlooks were very different in some ways, I liked and admired him.

When that little group of us sat round the table in the Justinlees bar, a mile up the road from Newbattle, over our beer, it was a kind of literary revivalist meeting, tinged with politics and (from Bill Drysdale) philosophy.

We left Newbattle in the high summer of 1952. Bob Fletcher had submitted an essay on Milton for the Cambridge University entrance examination. It was accepted, and Bob took his degree in English Literature there. (He had been preceded to King's College, Cambridge, the year before by Bill Drysdale, with a dissertation on Kant.) Ian MacArthur and Tom Wilson went to work in London, as clerks. Later Ian studied English Literature at Edinburgh University: he has recently retired from teaching at Forres, Morayshire. He married Edwin Muir's secretary, a lovely delightful girl called Flora Jack.

I followed him to Edinburgh University two years later.

There is no doubt that the influence of Edwin Muir and of those four fellow-students of mine helped to make me a writer. If I had stayed in Orkney, I would have gone on writing, to 'be for a moment merry' in the desert of boredom and poverty. But Newbattle stimulated me, and gave me a sense of purpose and direction.

I wrote some time later an impressionistic essay on Newbattle:

Newbattle

The city of Edinburgh: leaf-fall, 1951.

The silver-haired, soft-island-spoken poet waiting at Waverley in his car. Bold cliff of buildings, castle-crowned.

Trees, fertile fields; russet Autumn.

The Abbey, bordered with trees. Murmur of the River Esk. Stately heraldic entrance.

I am the third student. It is Sunday. Tomorrow the main body of students will flock in.

A high cold austere room: my dormitory.

The formal Italian garden: green Mozartian music. Great beech-tree beyond the hedge. The amazing octagonal sundial, a betrothal of mathematics and sculptured poetry.

Monday. All day the students came, Lowland Scots mostly, an Indian lecturer, a few English, an Italian economics lecturer.

A shyness, broken tentatively with poetry and politics, sometimes mixed. A left-wing group mostly, but none of the dour leveller ascetic kind.

Poetry, Labour, beer. A group emerged, including me. Yes, there was a pub a mile up the road, at Eskbank: Justinlees, 'jousting-in-the-leas', a medieval sports-field it must have been.

In the Justinlees we raised glasses for the first of a hundred times. Then the poetry came, eager and urgent.

Austere cold dormitories. (I had one to myself.) But rich abundant communal tables, thrice a day, and pleasant service.

At the high table the poet and his witty laughing wife, and the three other lecturers.

Lectures, small classes, in English Language and Literature, Politics, History, Philosophy, Economics.

I chose English and History.

Then the scanty but growing library, a sombre Calvinistic temple of learning. Dark desks, dark panelling.

You could write essays, make notes, strike a blank page ablaze with poetry! (Alas, most of what we wrote was scorching and soot in the cold light of morning.)

Next door, the magnificence of the drawing-room, azure and gilt ceiling, Van Dycks along the wall (the martyred soon-to-be-beheaded King), the grand piano where the poet's tall son Gavin Muir sketched Beethoven and Chopin, day after day.

Below, beside the wide stair-foot, the chapel, with a round Madonna and Child (school of Botticelli). The still beauty of the chapel was stirred only occasionally with curious breath.

The Abbey crypt was the common room. A big fireplace ablaze with logs. There, gravely, on the first night the poet–warden greets us all; he outlines the session ahead.

Winter darkened about us.

Bill sat up half the night writing a play that maybe had too much Bernard Shaw in it.

Tom wrote a story that the BBC accepted for broadcasting.

Everywhere, a spinning of webs; narrative and verse.

'Look, the *Observer* is having a Christmas Story competition' . . . we wrote Christmas stories. Flora, the secretary, typed them for us.

Bob distilled Milton and Melville into four intense lines.

A lecturer (Economics) had a poem in *The Listener*: Kenneth Wood.

Edwin, kindly, 'I'll see what I can do with the best of your poems.' I kindled. Flame of joy when the *New Statesman* accepted my poem 'The Exile'! And another flame, when *The Listener* (J. R. Ackerley) declined an offered poem, but asked to see more.

The quiet voice in the lecture room. Edwin, the poet–lecturer–warden, spoke from a few notes about Chapman or Marlowe or Ben Jonson.

The trees were bare, outside, soon.

We wandered beside the polluted mud-coloured river, under the cold winter sun.

We walked through the trees to Dalkeith. The people, I thought, looked grim. In the pubs, intense bitter arguments, obviously much enjoyed by the disputants. Tom was treating his half-dozen friends with the BBC cheque, perhaps. We kicked a football in the main street. A policeman ushered us into the police station. Tom answered him tartly, Bob dourly, I mumblingly. We were cautioned, let go.

At night, coming down the windy road from the Justinlees, the moon barged through the clouds 'like a rugby forward', said Tom.

Beside the great crypt fire, Shelley, Burns, Francis Thompson, Milton.

There was a ghost in the Abbey. A monk in love with a country girl. The house where they trysted, a torch was thrust into the thatch. The monk is met sometimes on the dark spiral winding up from the crypt. (I only dared that spiral in the light of summer.)

I think we all went home for Christmas with magic in our eyes.

Intense gray bitter frost, in January. Suddenly the heating failed.

Webster, caretaker, laboured to repair the wounded furnace, the Abbey heart.

Winter froze the Abbey. 'New Botyl': in medieval Newbattle the first coal in Scotland had been dug, black stones flowering into flame in the refectory. One or two old monks might have said, 'They have dug those black magic stones from the outworks of hell . . .'.

The Newbattle mines were exhausted long since. We crossed the river with saws, with axes. We cut down trees, sawed logs, every breath a long gray ghost. Then home with a hurdle of logs to the crypt as cold as a charnel; we sat round the hearth like souls yearning towards the purgatorial flame.

The blue hands in the library, turning the pages of Bradley, Kierkegaard, Keynes.

Thick mufflers and gloves in the lecture-hall, for *A Winter's Tale* or Trevelyan's *History*.

The garden creaked with frost and snow. The sundial was heaped with shadows.

Then in the heart of the great building the furnace was unblocked, the flames roared and danced about the boiler, the hot water gushed through the pipes.

We put our names down for baths – we who had washed

shiveringly, and shaved, in water that seemed to have blue slivers of ice in it . . .

Tom grew a great black beard, like an Assyrian.

Then the great storm in January. The massive beech-tree that had shadowed the garden from beyond the hedge was blown down.

The worst storm, said the radio, had hit the north and the islands. The poet listened with parted lips to the news of hen-houses blown out to sea. Willa Muir laughed at the story of the old maid's love letters blown by the wind hither and thither about an island.

'Come, a little get-together!' cried Willa. 'You must all come.' Inured to the crypt and the blank cold bedrooms, we admired the gracious flat the Muirs occupied.

It was Willa's evening. She set us down to savouries and sandwiches, cakes and wine. Her voice welcomed and mildly hectored and laughed to see the astonishment on our faces whenever she said something particularly satirical or outrageous (which was often).

The poet sat in a corner. He smiled, 'the blue flash in the eyes' that Willa wrote about later;* he crumbled a cake on his plate; he sent blue cigarette swirls about his head.

Willa's laughter and 'goodnights' followed us this way and that through the corridors to our cold rooms.

Word would come, 'Bring your essay to Dr Muir's study at noon.'

* *Belonging.*

High windows looking over the Italian garden. A haze of cigarette smoke. A few scrawled sheets on his desk: the essay. Kind quiet welcome. 'Come in, sit down . . .' He removes his glittering glasses to see the script, this particular piece of sapience concerning *Macbeth*. Silence. 'Oh, it's quite interesting . . . Do you think you're quite right here? I don't know . . .' A longer silence. 'You're happy enough here? Good. I'm glad . . .' He looks out through the window. Silence again, a wisdom deeper than words. 'What you've written is interesting. I like it . . .' I gather up the manuscript and depart.

Another student is waiting to go into the sanctum.

Somewhere in the Warden's desk is a drawer stuffed with manuscripts, the half-finished poems of *One Foot in Eden* perhaps . . . He must leave that trove for so many hours a week to comment on our barren scratchings.

Perhaps the light of his silence might awaken something, sometime.

Every Friday evening, a distinguished guest gives us a talk in the crypt. Professor MacMurray the philosopher, Professor Dover Wilson the Shakespearean, the minister from the kirk at the end of the long drive (local history), an Ayrshire lady on the Battle of Bannockburn, Norman MacCaig the Edinburgh poet on modern Scottish poetry, Alexander Scott on *The House with the Green Shutters*.

Also, recitals in the lovely gracious drawing-room: clarsach, piano, cello, by professional musicians from Edinburgh.

Spring stirring outside, in root and bud and the high villages of nests.

The little hoards of money we had brought – our council grants – were running out. Beer was one-and-twopence a pint, whisky a penny or two dearer.

Bill sold his Aran sweater for a pound. 'Bill, you could sell flowers from the garden on the streets of Dalkeith, sixpence a bunch . . .'

Cigarettes were dear, too.

There was no end to our hoards of poetry, brought from the ends of time. Only death would cancel those cargoes for us: strewn on strange shores, they are never lost. We hadn't chartered ship, requisitioned cargoes. Beachcombers we were, enchanted lingerers on the tidemark.

We waited for the perishable cheques to come from education authorities all over Scotland, at the beginning of each term.

News came to the literature class, 'The students of economics are to be conducted round Dalkeith brewery on such-and-such a day.'

We tumbled over ourselves to enrol as economics students (temporary).

A long table in the brewery was loaded with the firm's products: pale ale, export, strong ale, stout, lager.

After the tour – interesting for us drinkers – we fell like men in a desert on the oases of ales. We drank with a steady intensity.

Never were there such devoted economics students.

Next day we did not think of ourselves as called to the study of economics any more.

But we kept truth with beer and poetry.

In high spring, the bitter winter passed into me. I took to my bed in that cold high bare dormitory. The sword went in and left me sweating and shivering.

I went with Ian from Stornoway to stay with his brother Donald and his wife Kay and small daughter Anne in Paisley.

Orkney was too far away.

The town seemed seedy and worn ugly with industrialism, like a hopeless woman with twisted hands. Maybe I saw it that way because I was unwell. There must have been a score of towns in the industrial belt like Paisley.

The spirit of a town is in the people. Beauty and vitality flow through generations, however a town might change from a garden to a maze of sooty stone. Environment must be important, but the ever-renewing spring, brimming over in a community (laughter and lore) is not easily defiled, though factory chimneys rise.

I wrote light verse, read Neil Gunn, in Paisley. An old neighbour told of a man in Paisley or round about who had won the Irish Sweep, and told the crowd gathered at his front door they'd never want for a drink.

We went to Glasgow. I bought a pak-a-mac in Lewis's for ten shillings. We were bored by a film of *The Marriage of Figaro*. We went to Ayr races. I fancied a horse whose jockey was called De'Ath, but I was too poor to place a bet. The horse, De'Ath up, won.

One day I had a marvellous adventure. I got lost in Glasgow. I found my way to Paisley, alone, in the evening, by bus. They were worried about me.

The Clyde, the seagulls . . .

We went to the Citizen's Theatre to see *Juno and the Paycock*: a great play badly performed.

We saw a play, *Uranium 234*. At the interval I stood in the toilet stalls next to a kilted man with a terrier-head, Hugh MacDiarmid.

The loveliness of Newbattle in April.

The trees in blossom, lilac and apple and laburnum, on the long road – lyrical now – to the Justinlees.

We had shed winter skins.

Morning mists in the Esk valley; dispersing like ghosts towards noon.

We sat on the battlements with books and notes, in the sun.

'I think', said the poet, 'we'll have our class outside this morning . . .' He spoke, in his mild island voice, about the world's great books, *The Symposium*, Boswell's *Johnson*, *Don Quixote*; birdsong all around, and the Esk murmuring.

Ten weeks steeped in light and laughter.

The students very poor, after the grant was exhausted. (We had about £1 a week to spend.)

The tutors were not intimate with our small band of verse-and-beer men. Edwin and Willa approved of us. I got one or two mild queries from the poet: could it be right, drinking so much? The poetry: our love of poetry won his heart.

The beer-and-poetry men, when they were not in the Justinlees or the sun, drinking, communed with Milton and Kant in the library. The sons of Barleycorn drew light and beauty from Newbattle, more than the serious students did.

Willa emerged from the inner sanctum, to shed laughter on all troubles and strains. She was in pain much of the time with her arthritis.

Over the summer garden drifted from the drawing room sonata and prelude. Gavin Muir, away from music, devised mathematical formulae in proof of agnosticism. Gavin was first in the crypt when the morning newspapers came; he poured loud derision on Toryism and Liberalism; being deaf, he uttered his scorn straight out. The girl students smiled uneasily.

We went on a bus tour of the Borders, where the ballads were first uttered, Scotland's best literature. (Out of violence and anger those poems came: in the perfect society will no poetry be uttered: the people themselves will be syllables in the worldwide chorus of praise, the harmony of all created things.)

A day of happiness. Springtime in the spirit, springtime in the world, at one, inseparable.

One Sunday, a bus took us to the beach of Gullane. The sea and the sun. We had to spread camomile on our sore sun-pink shoulders that evening. That holiday too was rounded with happiness: 'desires falling across our bodies like blossoms . . .'.

Edwin's elegy for himself in *The Listener* one day: 'The Late Swallow', a perfect lyric.

Edwin's *Collected Poems* (1952) on the last day of the session.

The beer-and-verse men gave each other parting gifts: books we loved. I have Bob's *Billy Budd* still, that Edwin had inscribed to him.

We trooped with our cases, singly or in groups, from the great empty house and garden. Edwin and Willa bidding farewell from the entrance. It was mid June.

An idyll broken.

Never would be such pure happiness again: 'we few, we happy few . . .'.

But the time, immortal golden thread, was woven into us, not to be lost.

✧ ✧ ✧

After Newbattle, it was back to the desert again, living on National Assistance, lounging in bed till dinner-time (in Scotland the common people have their dinner about one p.m.) with books, sometimes writing a piece of a story or a play or poem. Every day I was one of the chorus in the pub. I didn't like darts or dominoes, only the beer and the stories and the laughter.

In 1953, the TB flared up again. This time I spent more than a year in the little sanatorium, Eastbank. There was a new medical officer, a young tall Scotsman called Dr Brodie. Dr Brodie, with the aid of the new powerful anti-TB drugs, streptomycin and PAS and INAH, was determined to clear Orkney of tuberculosis. It had been a scourge in the islands for a century perhaps; before that, I have been told, it was unknown in Orkney and Shetland. Many of the young island men went to sea, and brought the disease home. It went like wildfire through the defence-less populations. Whole families were wiped out in a few years. Conditions couldn't have been more favourable for the spread of the trouble. Families in the nineteenth century crowded together in small crofts, or in town houses. Clothes were handed down from brother to brother and sister to sister. Fresh air – especially the night air – was thought to be unhealthy, and so people lived in foetid rooms full of peat smoke and the smells of pigs and poultry.

By the mid twentieth century, living conditions had much improved, but the disease lingered on and killed its annual quota of people.

When I lay in Eastbank that second time, it was full of young men whose trouble had been detected in the early stages by mass radiography. Only one or two were really ill. Most of them wandered about in dressing-gowns, in high good spirits, or lay reading magazines and listening to transistors, taking their injections and capsules regularly. The PAS treatment consisted of swallowing about thirty large capsules daily. It wasn't so much my lungs as my stomach that troubled me; those healing capsules wrought havoc in the intestines.

Occasionally the patients got on each other's nerves. One day in winter a young patient put a handful of snow down my back. I hit out at him violently. Another patient with whom I was closeted in a two-bed ward had his transistor radio on much of the time. The pop music and manic voices that poured out enraged me so much that when one morning he was out of the ward for a little time I got out of bed and took the instrument and beat it violently against the wall. It was impossible to read or write while the ward brimmed with those dreadful sounds. I suppose I could have asked him to play it only when he *wanted* to hear a programme. But I have found that people are curiously insensitive to the nuisances they inflict on other people. The air is full of noises; sound is thought to be a natural and acceptable background in the twentieth century. Silence is the thing to be dreaded. But silence has always been precious to me.

I don't remember if I wrecked the transistor. I rather think not. Soon afterwards Dr Brodie spoke of starting a hospital magazine, and I was appointed editor. I said I would need the little ward with only one bed if I was to do the work properly. So, thankfully, elected silence 'beat upon my whorled ear'.

There were five or six issues of the hospital magazine, *Saga*, to which a surprising number of patients contributed, though I wrote most of the contents myself.

I must mention two of the older patients. One was a farmer from the parish of Rendall called Jimmy Sinclair, a small slight man with a heavy moustache. He was brought into the hospital desperately ill. But he soon revived, and I discovered one of the few really happy men I have known. Everything he had experienced in life he transmuted to laughter. There was a sweetness in his nature, so that it was a pleasure merely to be in his company.

For the Islands I Sing

The other patient I had deep affection for was a Kirkwall man called Davie Fox. He was a big burly man, and had been a municipal worker. Lying in bed irked him; all his life he had been up and stirring. He had quite a large family; somehow TB had touched one or two of his daughters (one mortally), and at last it had touched him. Davie Fox was a kind of father to the frustrated young Eastbank patients. They listened to his counsel. He had the ear too of the matron and the medical officer and the National Assistance officer who came to see to the patients' basic needs. He was straight and direct in his speech, as when he told the Assistance man to err on the generous side with clothing allowance to a young patient who was poor. (The same young man went for a lung operation to Aberdeen, and died on the table – a thing that shocked us by its suddenness, for in the weeks before going to Aberdeen he had been full of life and energy.) If there was any kind of quibbling or seeming parsimony in the officials, Davie Fox would remark tartly that most of the money for the poor went in administration, anyway. He was what some people would call a rough diamond, but I liked his honesty and straight talking, among many other good qualities. One day the matron's budgie flew out of the window and away. Davie Fox spent the best part of a day looking for the budgie, and at last found it in a nearby quarry. He had a reckless streak in his nature inherited from Irish ancestors. He was hardly out of hospital when he went to see the ritual game called 'the Ba'' that is played on the streets of Kirkwall each Christmas Day and New Year Day. He went as a spectator, but at last, remembering the Ba' games of his youth, he threw himself into the building scrum, and emerged some time later with cracked ribs. The recklessness was part of his generous nature.

Davie Fox and Jimmy Sinclair came to be the greatest of friends, and I was admitted into their company. We had one happy day at Jimmy's farm of Lyking in Rendall.

Both those good men are dead now. I remember them with gratitude and affection.

In the great battle against TB that went on the 1950s, there was the pneumo-thorax treatment, in which the diseased lung was put out of action by injecting air into the rib-cage. I was not thought to be a suitable case for pneumo-thorax. There were more drastic operations that involved the cutting of ribs; but for that the patient had to go to the specialist surgeons in Aberdeen. It was thought that I might be a case for such saving butchery, and so I was flown to Woodend Hospital for tests. Woodend is a huge hospital. The large echoing ward they put me in was full of mostly young men, and there was constant coming and going of nurses, doctors, cleaners, patients, visitors. The bed next to me was occupied by a young Shetlander, who spoke in such a broad accent that the staff had difficulty in understanding him. It was easier for me, though the speech of Orkney and Shetland is quite different; Shetlandic is nearer to the original Norse. One day screens were put round the bed of the Shetlander, and a Polish doctor came to give him a 'bronchoscopy'. Some kind of viewing instrument is pushed down the throat, and the examining doctor can actually look into the lungs. After some time the doctor departed with his instrument and the screens were taken away. The Shetland man lay immobile and speechless in his bed, and made no reply when I asked him how he did? At last, after some hours, he found his voice. 'Oh,' said he, 'yon bronchoscopy! . . .' And after another while he said, 'I never in all my life had such an experience as yon bronchoscopy.' His voice was full of dread and amazement. 'Pray', he said after another long silence, 'that du never hes dat bronchoscopy done tae dee!'

In the end I didn't have to endure either the bronchoscopy or the rib-cutting operation, and was flown home to my quiet ward in the little island sanatorium.

I was discharged in the summer of 1954, once more into the desert.

A few months later my eldest brother Hughie suffered the first of the series of heart attacks that killed him in March 1956. This sickness of his was a shock to all the community, for he had always seemed so fit and strong, and was well-liked. He was steward of the local British Legion Club.

I always associate his first heart attack with the writing of a short story of mine called 'Tam': did they happen on the same day perhaps? I wrote it at one go, very quickly, sitting on a bench on the hill behind Stromness, near a farm called Quildon. The story came singing off the pen, and the *Orkney Herald* published it, and later *The New Shetlander*. It was the first-written story in my collection *A Calendar of Love*. The writing of such a piece infuses a mingling of sweetness and power, difficult to convey. It is quite unlike any other kind of pleasure.

✧ ✧ ✧

I had written short stories before 'Tam', of course, but I would not like my eye to chance on them now. I have written many since. It might be of interest to note, in passing, that my best stories have nearly always come fluently and required little correction. Keats had said in a letter that poems should come as naturally as leaves upon a tree. With other stories I have had almighty struggles, which have lasted for days, weeks, months. While the battle went on, I would console myself that this was how art ought really to be created, in sweat and blood. It is part of the Scottish ethic that everything worthwhile must be grimly fought for. I think for me this is not so, but I know that many writers do achieve their best work by hard toil.

It is a curious experience, to be locked in hard struggle with a story or a poem. After a session, when the manuscript resembles a battlefield and only a few words or sentences have emerged, one part of the mind says, 'Ah, that was worthwhile – these few phrases were worth all that smithy-toil. Keep at it till it's finished!' The true spirit whispers, 'No – it's worse than it was before. You've got yourself into a fine mess. Leave it alone for a while.'

When seemingly insoluble difficulties arise, I have learned to break off the battle at once. Put the manuscript away in a drawer and leave it for weeks or months. Then, when you look at it again, you see at once where the story or the poem began to go wrong, beyond any argument. The subconscious mind – or the spirit of art – has been working on the problem in secrecy and silence, while the conscious mind was busy about lesser things. I do not believe what Shakespeare's fellow-actors reported to Ben Jonson, that Shakespeare 'never blotted line'. But I can understand how such a mind moved from image to image, from character to character, from scene to scene, effortlessly.

❖ ❖ ❖

After the death of my brother Hughie I fell into one of those troughs of depression that have irked me from time to time; and still persist.

Then I remembered that I still had in my keeping a term's grant for Newbattle that hadn't been used up. I wrote to the new Warden, Edwin Muir's successor, and was accepted for the summer term. Again, it was a happy time; the students were different in kind from those of four years previously, quieter and soberer and more earnest in their quest for knowledge (but less brilliant). There were some delightful people among them. I fell in love, I thought, briefly, with a girl student from Aberdeen. There was one disastrous evening. I had written a talk on Edwin Muir and was asked to record it at the BBC studio in Queen Street, Edinburgh. The producer was a pleasant man, a well-known modern Scottish poet: George Bruce. To give me courage, I had a few drams before I went to read the script.

I invited a fellow-student Edward McLaughlan to come with me in the bus from Dalkeith to Edinburgh. The talk in the studio didn't go well; the sight of the microphone, and the technicians behind the glass screen, all but paralysed my tongue. At the end of it I was given a cheque for something over £9. Then Eddie and I went on the spree, first in the Rose Street pubs, I think, and later in the Justinlees at Eskbank. It was two woefully drunken figures who turned in at the Abbey gates later that evening and staggered down the long drive. As it happened, that evening the college was entertaining a group of colonial students from Edinburgh University; in the hope, I think, of impressing them so much that when they got home to Jamaica, Ghana, etc., they would let it be known what good things Newbattle had to offer, and so induce sorely-needed new students to enrol. The two drunk students arrived, rising and falling, just as the colonial students were about to leave on their bus. The carefully planned visit was a ruin. Next morning, when I was sitting wretched with hangover in the library, the new college secretary arrived to tell me that the new Warden wished to see me at once in his office. I was curtly told to pack my bags and go. Edward McLaughlan was let off with a severe reprimand. I was considered to be the chief culprit, and so I was.

Still, I was stunned and shaken by this expulsion.

Then those earnest and quiet students went into action, led by a young left-wing student of politics called Max Flood. Max Flood organised the students and said that if I had to go, they would all leave the college. Furthermore, he would see to it that there were reporters and photographers from the *Daily Mail* present at the great walk-out.

Fortunately for us all, there was a peacemaker in the student body, an ordained Church of Scotland minister, the Revd James Campbell, a native of Caithness. James was a man of diplomatic skills. He went, carrying the palm branch, between the Warden's office and the crypt. At that day's end I was reprieved, but on the understanding that for the rest of my time at Newbattle I would never darken the door of the Justinlees or any other pub. I kept to my part of the bargain.

May and June passed like a dream. I was increasingly infatuated with the girl from the north-east; I remember murmuring 'Shall I compare thee to a summer's day . . .' into her ear one night. These were hours of great happiness. (Shakespeare was better at love language than me.)

✧ ✧ ✧

Sometime that summer term, between the expulsion and the last lyrical days beside the Esk, I thought it would be particularly dreadful to go back into the desert without that compass and chart that Scotsmen consider necessary for the achievement of a good life. I applied to become a student of English Literature at Edinburgh University. I had acquired all the necessary qualifications at school in Stromness, including Higher Latin. The Warden, with whom I had been on uneasy terms, backed me with a good reference. In due course I was accepted, and the Orkney Education Committee gave me a grant.

I am grateful for my four years at Edinburgh University. Not only did I make a host of friends – 'friends that have been friends indeed' – but gates were opened into fresh fields of knowledge. Two or three hundred of us first-year students flowed each morning into large lecture halls where, for example, Professor John MacMurray lectured on Moral Philosophy. I sat there, quite enchanted. University history was not like school history; I learned to see people and events in the round, compelled by the pressures of the period they lived in, both free and fated, I chose to think. Old English and Middle English dismayed me to begin with, but once I had broken the code (the difficult Anglo-Saxon grammar) I delighted in *Beowulf* and *The Seafarer* and *The Battle of Maldon* and King Alfred's prose. There were lectures, too, of unutterable pedantry. Our small tutorial group was presided over by a delightful elderly scholar called Dr George Kitchin, who (I think) had been brought back from retirement. He punctuated our stammering efforts to grasp the riches of literature with salty benign remarks. He would praise the beer brewed in the brewery just below our high tutorial window in Minto Street, where we were supposed to be deep into Pope or Chaucer. Sometimes he seemed to drift off into a light sleep, but would wake soon, his mind vivid with the rhythms and images we were splurging in: a dozen or so mature boys and girls; and I the oldest one among them, a kind of stepping-stone between themselves and the sceptical wisdom of Dr Kitchin. He seemed like one of those eighteenth-century Edinburgh eccentrics, strayed into the wrong century. By way of an essay, I showed Dr Kitchin some of my recent poems, and he gave me such high marks that I'm sure it elevated me into second position in the class of about three hundred, when the total session's achievements were reckoned.

I was homesick for Orkney during my first few weeks in Edinburgh. But friend by friend by friend appeared; at the end of four years there was a host of them, most of them true and generous and reliable, a few astonishing characters that seemed to have come full-fleshed out of some brilliant farce.

When I think of Edinburgh in the late 1950s, so many scenes and events and characters come flooding back that I know it is impossible to write about all of them. Not impossible; they remain fascinating to me; but I lack the skill to convey to a reader their full unique essence.

Some fleeting impressions will have to do.

I lodged in an area of Edinburgh called Marchmont, a Victorian spread of tenements separated from the main city by a great open park called The Meadows. Hundreds of students lived in the district – a ten-minute walk after breakfast brought them to the main part of the University, the 'Old Quad', with the halls and old refurbished churches that stood about it like satellites to house the ever-expanding number of students and subjects. The University was scattered all over the city. The Old Quad, that had once housed all the faculties, was being used increasingly for administration. It was a widely-admired Adam structure from the eighteenth century; I was shocked by the ingrained filth of the stonework, and also by the grimy exterior of the National Gallery in Princes Street. In Orkney, all the buildings were clean, scoured by salt wind and rain.

Unlike the other students, I rarely walked across The Meadows. Every ten minutes or so a municipal bus stopped briefly just outside the door of 23 Marchmont Crescent, and it bore me most mornings to the top of Chamber Street, only a minute's walk from the lecture-halls. After two or three years of bus-riding, one of my student friends John Durkin used to say that one of those buses belonged to me, I had paid so many fares. (It was not so much laziness as my scarred lungs; walking even a short distance was a burden.)

I was amazed by the dryness of Edinburgh. In Orkney, in autumn and winter, it rains at least every second day. In Edinburgh weeks seemed to pass without a drop of rain.

All my life I have been fortunate in the number and variety of rich characters I have known. My chief landlady, by far the most memorable one of four or five, was Mrs Margaret Thomson of Marchmont. She was an indomitable woman who brooked no nonsense from anyone, high or low. Her life had been so clouded by misfortunes that most women would have been soured or broken. Her husband had died in the terrible 'flu after the First World War. Her two daughters had died young, one of TB and one of food-poisoning. She had such extraordinary vitality and humour that those piteous events, though never forgotten – she often spoke about them – had somehow been gathered into the loom of her days, and she had acquired a tranquillity, a formal acceptance.

Mrs Thomson was an elderly woman when I stayed with her, and almost blind. She loved the company of students, and the further away they came from the better she seemed to like it. I think she nearly always had a black student in residence – 'he's black's the lum' (chimney) she would confide to visitors.

Mrs Thomson belonged to the town of Fraserburgh, near Aberdeen, where her father had been a harbour-master; 'Lang Rob' had been his nickname. She still spoke in such a rich broad Aberdeenshire accent that I doubt whether most of her lodgers understood what she was saying. But we all rejoiced in the fun she radiated all day and every day.

But at any misdemeanour she blazed up and her rage came at you, straight from the shoulder. I got a blistering reprimand from her for coming home merry with drink one night from a Sunday bus-outing to St Andrews. Next morning the slate was washed clean: we were friends again in a world at peace – and a world that was almost certain to blossom with drollery of some kind before the sun was down.

In the butcher shop on the ground floor right under Mrs Thomson's flat, some years before, a support had buckled suddenly. There was a possibility that one section of the tenement would collapse. The room where Mrs Thomson kept a student was sealed off (it was the same room that I was to occupy a few years later). The weak support was buttressed; all was well. There followed legal arguments, about cost, responsibilities, etc. It seemed to Mrs Thomson that the depositions were dragging on in a Dickensian way. At last she rose up in the courtroom – though it was unprecedented – and delivered herself of a passionate ringing speech in her broad Buchan dialect – a feat for which she received the court's congratulations. In the end the case was settled satisfactorily. This incident I heard often, and I never tired of it. She was that kind of woman. She was afraid of nothing. She would bring to any entanglement, practical or personal or professional, a sharp-edged common-sense . . . then, after a brief interval, the incident was seen as part of life's comedy.

We got on famously.

She was so purblind when I was her lodger that perhaps she ought not to have had the care of students at all. I think she was afraid of loneliness, inactivity, the last shrivellings. But she looked after her three students well – a black dental student from British Honduras, a Norwegian engineering student, and myself. I'm sure no trio of students ever lived in such a web of strength and laughter.

When she wanted a letter written, she would invite me into her kitchen to write it at her dictation.

Mrs Thomson had once belonged to the Women's Orange Order, an offshoot of the Northern Irish one named after William of Orange.

In the 1930s there had been a strong anti-Catholic movement in Edinburgh, set going by a bitter-tongued man called John McCormack who used to speak at the Mound, Edinburgh's open-air arena, on Sunday afternoons, guarded by a bunch of toughs. It was the nearest Scotland ever came to Fascism, with Catholics instead of Jews as the scapegoats. My landlady had left the order in anger and disgust when she heard McCormack's jeering remarks about a boat-load of Irish fisher-folk who had been drowned in a storm returning, I think, from the herring-fishing in Scotland. Mrs Thomson had in her youth worked beside those Irish fish-girls; she had got to know and love them.

I heard McCormack speaking once at the Mound. A Catholic Edinburgh girl called Margaret Sinclair had in the earlier part of this century become a Poor Clare nun; word of her devout life had seeped through from the closed walls of her English convent, after her early death, and had put wonderment on the Catholics of Scotland. McCormack's open-air sermon that Sunday afternoon was one long bitter sneer at Margaret Sinclair. 'Why,' he cried, 'her father was *a scaffy*! (lowland Scots for a scavenger, or street cleaner).' It was that dreadful sentence that stuck in my mind.

But by the late 1950s McCormack's influence had waned. I never experienced any anti-Catholic feelings in Edinburgh. The students whose company I relished were Catholics; I think especially of John Durkin, a philosophy student and an ex-Newbattleite. In his house I experienced the closeness and kindness of Catholic family life. His mother was like one of those generous indomitable women that Sean O'Casey writes about in his plays. Catholicism was worked into the texture of their lives: it wasn't the kind of self-conscious piety that is often to be found in respectable Presbyterian households, for there was no objection to drink and fun (so long as they were kept within bounds). There was a wild free Irish extravagance in John Durkin's gaiety that leavened any dour Scottish company he found himself in. And yet we had quiet serious talks together, and we troubled with delight the deep waters of poetry and speculation.

John Durkin no longer went to Mass, but when one has been bred a Catholic, one can never rid oneself of the essence of it. A cradle Catholic is quite different from a convert. Textures of Calvinism, generations old, are still part of me and I think I will never be rid of them: ancient guilts, rebukes in the silence of thought, or when I am reading or writing, weigh on the heart, as if some Presbyterian ancestor from the seventeenth century was murmuring to me, and not mildly.

I have just mentioned Scottish 'dourness' – the hackneyed epithet applied to the Scots, in England especially. This seriousness of mind is on the surface, mainly. I remember telling Willa Muir when I first went to Newbattle that I had never known in Orkney such grim faces as I met on the streets of Dalkeith. The typical Orkney face is open and gentle in comparison. And when I went into the Dalkeith pubs – the first places I sought out, of course – the difference in the atmosphere was striking. Whereas in the Orkney pubs talk tended always towards reminiscence and story, here all was argument, and deep almost passionate argument. Men would glare at each other and thump their fists on the bar. It was only gradually that I came to understand that the verbal strife was an enjoyment to them; out of such fierce threshings of thought arose the great Scottish philosophers, as great poetry is rooted in the vivid speech of illiterate peasants the world over.

As for that other cliché, the humourlessness of the Scots, that is false too. In my experience, it is a deeper richer humour than the light squibs and japes of the English. (Here, too, I know I am guilty of generalisation – Falstaff and Chaucer's pilgrims and Tristam Shandy were made out of rich laughing dust. I am judging on poor evidence – the endless English comedy series on TV, half a dozen or so a week, that seem such thin frail futile stuff.) But the humour of the Scottish working class is wonderful to listen to – and there they are every day in every pub in Edinburgh, those rich dark verbal clashings, while the combatants glare at each other over their beer in a deep conspiratorial joy. This different style of humour took me some time to get used to.

More than the lecture halls of the university, it was the pubs that drew me. In my first rootless days in Edinburgh, I remember sitting in a pub near the Old Quad called Greyfriars Bobby, having a warm pie and a pint of beer for lunch, and reading Bede's *History of England*, one of the set books. There was an image, in the foreword, of the old monk sitting in the bitter cold of his monastery writing on his parchment by candle-light. The image enthralled me; and yet I felt as isolated and cold as Bede, while the students – all strangers yet – came and went in scores and hundreds. Boy students and girl students drifted about hand-in-hand, a thing never known in Orkney. I envied them.

A certain street in Edinburgh, Rose Street, I had heard
about many a time. Once, they said, there had been forty
pubs in that long dingy chasm; now they had shrunk to
fourteen. And there prostitutes came out at night, like
moths. (But I wasn't interested in them. Once a rather
withered woman that I took to be a prostitute had made a
vague gesture towards me, and I had made haste to get
away.) Certain of the Rose Street pubs – The Abbotsford,
Milne's Bar – were the meeting-places of Scottish writers.
I had read MacDiarmid, MacCaig, Sydney Goodsir Smith,
Tom Scott, in various collections. It seemed wonderful that
soon I should see them, and maybe overhear their
conversation; there was no chance that I would ever be able
to speak to them.

The Abbotsford is a handsome spacious bar, a relic of
the Victorian age. The circular counter is an island in the
centre of the bar, richly gantried with all the drinks of the
western world, especially whiskies. And there, one Friday
night, they were, in a cluster at one corner of the counter,
Norman MacCaig and Sydney Goodsir Smith and a few of
their friends. Simply to be there, watching that famous
huddle, was a delight. I drank my beer but dared not go
near them . . . The same scene, with different groups of
writers and artists, was repeated over the weeks and
months that followed.

Sydney Goodsir Smith: whether it was that he had
noticed my perpetual timid hoverings in their vicinity, or
whether he had been told that I had been at Newbattle
under Edwin Muir, I don't know, but one day he crossed
over and spoke to me, and invited me to join the group.

I was so confused that I shook my head; I would stay where I was. And yet the fact that he had spoken to me was a joy. After the poet had rejoined his friends, I could have kicked myself. In time, however, and in my own devious way, I drifted into the company of the Rose Street poets, and got a civil acceptance.

I mention this act of Sydney Goodsir Smith by way of paying tribute to his kindness. Outside of Scotland his poetry is hardly known, because it was written entirely in Scots, in the language of Dunbar and Henryson and Burns and the early MacDiarmid. His best lyrics are magnificent. He wrote a sequence of love poems, *Under the Eildon Tree*, that is one of the great works of the twentieth century. In any other culture, those poems would have brought him instant lasting fame. One Englishwoman saw what magnificent stuff they were: Edith Sitwell. She hailed Sydney, as she had hailed Dylan Thomas while he was still far off.

Such a cold reception for such fine poetry would have embittered some poets. Not Sydney. He tasted life and literature with great gusto, like one of the medieval wandering scholars. He delighted in other people. Though he was not a religious man, he had the kind of charity that St Paul speaks of. I never heard him say a bitter or a cruel word about anyone. Under all the laughter and boisterousness, he was a kind gentle man.

He stemmed from the upper professional classes. His father was Sir Sydney Smith, Professor of Forensic Medicine at Edinburgh University. For a while Sydney studied medicine at Edinburgh, and afterwards history, I think, at Brasenose College, Oxford. But study was irksome to him. He was a poet, and he knew it, and to poetry he would devote his life.

It seems strange that he, who spoke in an upper-class English voice, wrote his poetry in Scots. Language and genius have their own mysterious ways with a poet and Sydney must have drawn his poetry from deep ancestral roots.

He had only limited fame in his lifetime. I am sure that his genius will be acknowledged some day. Today the tide seems set against the culture – especially the poetry – of small nations. A great gray universal language at last might cover everything. But I have a kind of faith that a people's language is more closely related to the mountains and seas and rivers than we now think; natural forms and sounds and silences begetting poetry. The 'little white rose of Scotland' is perdurable as schist.

Like Dr Kitchin, Sydney Goodsir Smith was an eighteenth-century Edinburgh man. Claret should have been his drink, not whisky and pints of Export beer. His true place was with Fergusson and Smollett and Boswell.

Norman MacCaig was a Rose Street poet too, whose early work I had got to know before I went to Edinburgh. Beautifully and intricately wrought poems they are; I think of the artistry of a master-jeweller. His early poems were patterned into rhyme and stanza; what beguiled the reader were sudden brilliant flashes of imagery. The connections had been there, all the time; it was the hawk eye of the poet that could see those startling similes, those 'rhymes' and 'puns' and imitations and camouflages in nature that make a harmony in the complete web. Later, MacCaig abandoned strict verse forms for freer modes. But, as T. S. Eliot remarks, 'no verse is free for the man who wants to do a good job'. On the contrary, to write 'free verse' is extremely difficult; the poet must have an impeccable ear and sense of rhythm, otherwise the thrust and flow of his poem peters out in a marsh. The first begetter of free verse, Walt Whitman, had the necessary gifts to bring it off, often magnificently; so had D. H. Lawrence, Eliot, Pound, Edith Sitwell. MacCaig brought mastery to this most difficult form, too. Writing of birds and animals, he had Keats's ability to enter into them and take part in their existence.

People have held it against MacCaig that there is a cold-ness in his art, little of the human sympathy that is a nec-essary part of poetry. One has only to read the sequence of elegies written on the sudden death of a friend of his, a countryman from the north-west of Scotland, to hear the *lachrymae rerum*. Again, the images are brilliant, the grief held in perfect control; but only a man of deep feeling could have struck and held the pure elegiac note.

Norman MacCaig held open house, especially at week-ends, to writers and artists and their friends. He was a generous host, and his wife Isobel was too, a quiet serene intelligent woman. Whisky and anecdote and literary matters flowed till well into Saturday morning. Those parties at Leamington Terrace happened so often that when I try to remember them they seem woven into a single tapestry with Bacchus and Apollo turning to one another, their beakers touching. Many a Friday night, after 'time-up' had been called at Milne's Bar or The Abbotsford, a bus would fill up with writers and artists and their friends going to MacCaig's with their 'cairry-oots' – that is, their contribution to the party, which might be a bottle of whisky or two screwtops of pale ale, or anything between.

Some weekends, nearly all the writers of Scotland seemed to be guests at Leamington: Sydney Goodsir Smith, Tom Scott, Alan Riddell, Charles Senior, the publisher Callum MacDonald and the librarians John Broom and Harry Taylor, and a shifting host of people who liked books and writers and artists.

Occasionally the great king of Scottish letters, the poet Hugh MacDiarmid, came to spend the weekend from his home near Biggar in Lanarkshire. I was chary of MacDiarmid, to begin with, because I could not get out of my mind the violence of his repeated assaults on Edwin Muir. They had been good friends back in the 1920s – MacDiarmid had dedicated to Muir one of his best lyrics – but in the early 1930s Edwin Muir published a book called *Scott and Scotland*, in which he attacked the corner-stone of MacDiarmid's plan for the building of a Scottish literary renaissance; 'literary Scots' was to oust English, as the language enshrining the true spirit of a people. MacDiarmid, himself born only three or four miles from the English border, had listed 'anglophobia' in *Who's Who* among his chief preoccupations. Muir said in his book that the time had come for Scottish writers to accept the fact that now they could only do their best work in English. From then on their ways divided: on one side the fruitful stream, on one the roaring cataract. Again and again MacDiarmid hurled his rage at Muir. Muir was not a

Scottish writer at all, he said, but an Orcadian writer. (This, in a sense, was true. Though Orkney had been a part of Scotland for 500 years, the Scots tongue was alien north of the Pentland Firth; and though Muir had attempted one or two early ballad-poems in Scots, he quickly realised that he could do his best work in English. He had been too long out of the islands to write in the Orkney dialect like Robert Rendall, and by the time he had begun to write seriously he was drawing on the whole of European culture for sustenance. In fact, Muir wrote beautiful pellucid English, both poetry and prose; English was not a foreign language to him at all.)

Edwin Muir was hurt by those attacks on him by one who had been a friend. Among his other gifts, MacDiarmid was a master of invective. He had called Muir, for example, 'a paladin in mental fight, with the presence of Larry the Lamb', a reference to Muir's natural gentleness, and to his refusal, after stating his position with regard to Scottish writers and the language they ought to use, to engage in prolonged and violent 'flyting' with MacDiarmid . . . I think they did indeed meet once, towards the end of Muir's life, in a BBC studio discussion, and appeared to get on tolerably well. But there was no true reconciliation.

I had been prepared, on first meeting MacDiarmid, to find the same kind of man who expressed himself with such violence in his essays and articles. And would I dare to say that I was an Orkneyman? I found myself talking to a quiet courteous humorous man, who listened attentively to my half-baked opinions and observations, and showed nothing but encouragement and goodwill.

For the Islands I Sing

He ought perhaps to have been a bitter man (and the way Scotland had treated him in his first beginnings as a poet might have been responsible for the anger of his prose), because his early poetry is drenched with genius, and his reward was neglect, poverty, a year-long exile in the island of Whalsay in Shetland. *Sangschaw* and *Penny Wheep* were his first books of lyrics in Scots: magnificent short poems that combine delight in the wild natural life and the extraordinary characters or 'bodies' that have always inhabited the country places of Scotland, with a kind of cosmic vision: common dust and the wheel of galaxies are one. Earth is an 'eemis stane'. The planets are like beautiful girls dressed for a country fair and gossiping to each other. 'The auld mune shaks her gowden feathers . . .'. Those two books of lyrics were followed by a long poem, *A Drunk Man Looks at the Thistle*, a marvellous meditation, in many styles, on the state of Scotland and what should be Scotland's true place in the comity of nations. Humour, satire, passion, religion and politics, pure lyricism meet and mingle in this work which is another of the great poems of the twentieth century. But again, because it is written in Scots, it is hardly known outside Scotland; and the famous critics like Leavis who are supposed to weigh everything in the balance, and know the pure gold from the dross, take no account of it. It is possible that, if the poem was shorter, the world's readers might have turned its pages and discovered the wonder of it. If Ezra Pound had been at hand with his scissors to do for *A Drunk Man* what he had done for *The Waste Land* . . . It is impossible to say; if treasures are laid up in

128

heaven, then MacDiarmid will have his reward. But while the treasures were being wrought and offered on earth, he had a hard time of it.

His extraordinarily subtle mind could contain contradictions which other folk found baffling. He called himself an atheist, and yet God and Christ and Bethlehem come into his poetry again and again. He was both a Communist and a Scottish Nationalist; it was said he was expelled from the Communist party for his nationalism, and from the Nationalist party for his Communism. When Russian tanks rolled into Hungary in 1956, and the British Communists were leaving the party in droves, MacDiarmid promptly rejoined it. Scots, he proclaimed over and over, was 'the only language for a Scottish writer'. But in his massive later poems, *In Memoriam James Joyce* and *The Kind of Poetry I Want*, he writes in English. It is almost as difficult to read those long poems as it is to read Pound's *Cantos*. But every now and again he breaks out into passages of marvellous controlled eloquence. The stone in his hand becomes a bird. But mostly in those great quarries of verse it is stone, stone, stone, until the mind grows tired.

Another paradoxical event happened late in MacDiarmid's life. Ezra Pound was living in Venice, having been released from the mental institution in his native America into which he had been hustled for supporting Mussolini, and broadcasting propaganda on the Italian radio all through the war. MacDiarmid and his wife Valda were driven across Europe to Venice by their friends Kulgin Duval and Colin Hamilton, and there one day the

Communist poet and the Fascist poet met gravely, and walked and talked together. Apart from being poets, a tenuous thread connected them. They both subscribed, to some extent at least, to an economic theory called Social Credit, first propounded by a man called Major Douglas, and actually put into practice in the 1930s – with what results I do not know – in the province of Alberta, Canada.

Kulgin Duval and Colin Hamilton published some of MacDiarmid's later poems, in superbly produced editions. They proved to be good friends to me also, first in their high flat in Rose Street, later in Falkland in Fife, and later still at their beautifully restored steading on the shore of Loch Tummel, Perthshire.

MacDiarmid is certainly one of the major figures of all Scottish literature, and I think probably our greatest poet since Burns.

✧ ✧ ✧

In this beautiful city of Edinburgh I lived for six years, except for holiday-times in Orkney. I came to love it, especially in that enchanting time between Easter and midsummer, when the trees clothe themselves in green and the fountain leaps in the garden under the Castle Rock, and the lyrical geometry of the flower-beds compels the citizens and students. Time is told in flowers in the steep earth-set clock. The statues between Princes Street and the Gardens lose much of their solemnity. The one of Sir Walter Scott sits in the eye of his grimy sky-soaring needle. There is laughter of children in the heart of the capital, and young couples commune on the grass, and students turn the pages of their books (for the degree exams are only a few weeks away) under the trees. Gray doves are everywhere, and they don't need to worry about their next meal, for the whole world conspires to feed them.

It was fortunate that I quite enjoyed studying, even such an alien subject as Moral Philosophy. One of the set books was Kant's *Groundwork to a Metaphysics of Morals* (that's of course the English title). I took one affrighted look at the first few paragraphs, and my head reeled. There was not a possibility that I would ever understand such stuff. Somehow I got hold of a commentary by a Jesuit priest, Fr Copleston, on Kant's book. The commentary dispelled the dense Germanic fogs. I enjoyed Copleston, and so managed to answer the exam question on Kant when the time came. But now even the commentary has faded. The Scottish fascination with philosophy – Kant himself had Scottish ancestors – never rubbed off on me. Hume was incomprehensible too, and boring. The fault is in myself; I have known fine minds who have been enthralled life-long by Hume, and by other philosophers, even the difficult modern ones. The minds of writers work in a different way, in pulsing controlled image sequences, which are no less strict than the workings of music or mathematics or philosophy.

One session – two exams – and we were quit forever of history and moral philosophy. For the next three years forty or fifty of us had to concentrate on English Literature and English Language.

There comes now a question that can't be avoided – how is it possible to teach English literature? I had seen in the classrooms in Stromness how the force-feeding of 'important books' can set the delicate minds of children against literature for ever.

But here, at university, it would be, surely, an altogether different matter. The class of young men and women I found myself in, they were there because they loved books and literature and wanted to devote their lives to it. (Most of them would become teachers at the end of the course.) We found many of our older lecturers dull and boring – a generation brings such revaluations; one could almost see them blowing the cobwebs off textbooks. 'All shuffle there, all cough in ink/All wear the carpet with their shoes . . .'. But there were young lecturers too, bright-eyed and eloquent, looking at centuries-old classics from a new exciting viewpoint, and even venturing into *The Waste Land* and beyond. I heard brilliant lectures on Eliot, Yeats, Edith Sitwell, Muir (names and achievements that were anathema to at least one of the older lecturers, who almost snarled their names as if they were bitter personal enemies: whereat the young students clapped enthusiastically for those heroes of twentieth-century poetry, and the lecturer, in his exile, 'coughed in ink' towards the end of another dry-as-dust lecture).

I think the best that is done in the English Literature department of a university is the sudden illumination that gifted lecturers can shed on old books. The old books themselves are always changing, always yielding new beauties and truths. The pristine flashes off a hitherto hidden facet of the work. Bad books are prisoned in their own time – a touch, and they fall to dust. A good book belongs to all ages, it is an oasis of water and greenery, it is watched over by its own generous spirit. That spirit welcomes people of a shallow and sordid time even more kindly than it welcomed the first readers of Chaucer, Shakespeare, Wordsworth: because we have more need of the nourishment.

I am sure that many of my classmates left enriched after four years. And so, in a way, did I: though I took most of my treasure from Old English and Middle English.

In general, I do not *like* books. To be given a list of set books to study at the start of each university session set up an immediate resistance – the same kind of blockage that Sir Walter Scott induced at school. I read the six novels of Jane Austen without delight, and wondered why such a really great novelist as Forster admired her deeply. Edwin Muir, too, had told me that whenever he was depressed, he found balm and solace in Jane Austen. Her characters seemed to me like creatures from another artificial planet where life as I had observed it in Orkney meant nothing: barren, effete, rootless. (As I write this, I know I am exposing my shortcomings and denseness. But one must be honest.)

Some of the young lecturers at Edinburgh held the name of the Cambridge critic Leavis in high regard. I had, years before, read a book by him on the modern poets, especially Eliot and Hopkins and Pound, and that book had been an eye-opener. But now Leavis had gone stale on me, and sour. I found his prose contorted and difficult. I read an essay on

Forster, and it angered me. To have those treasures – *Where Angels Fear to Tread*, *A Room with a View*, *A Passage to India* – trodden underfoot so contemptuously: it was too much, I closed that Leavis book and have never opened it or another by him since. But there is no doubt that Leavis at Cambridge must have been a great illuminator, since a whole generation of his students paid him such homage.

In the end it must come to this: the enjoyment of a book is a purely subjective experience, and can never be 'taught'. Everything depends on the hunger of the reader. To think one likes a book because a critic or scholar has said it has merit is a kind of small betrayal.

I should say honestly that I did not read all the set books. Looking back over examination papers from previous years, I was frequently puzzled by the relevance of the questions to the poem or play or novel. Those questions had nothing to do with what I found intriguing or exciting in them, and so I didn't see how I could have tackled the question in an exam. And if they seemed irrelevant to works that I enjoyed, what on earth would I make of questions about books that I found tedious? In the past few decades there had grown up a forest of critical studies on all the 'important' works of English literature, from *Beowulf* to *The Waste Land*, many of them well argued and well written. Penguin Books was always pouring out such studies, no doubt for students like me. I am truly ashamed to say it, but in many instances I neglected the set texts and read what clever contemporary university men had to say about them. (In the same way Fr Copleston had helped me with Kant.)

But certain doors were opened to me. At the beginning of our second year a new head of department, Professor Butt, came to Edinburgh, and gave a series of impressive lectures on eighteenth-century literature. Up to that time, the eighteenth century had not been a happy hunting ground for me, apart from bits of Pope ('At Timon's villa let us pass a day . . .') and *The Deserted Village* and bits of Cowper, and, of course, the incomparable Burns. John Butt showed us many riches in what I had thought to be a dry century.

I think it was a woman lecturer, Winifred Maynard, who quickened us to the poetry of Donne and Herbert. Donne, after centuries of neglect, had been 'rediscovered' in this same university by Professor Herbert Grierson, a Shetlander. His *Anthology of Metaphysical Poetry* is an abiding delight. This is what true scholarship should be.

A few years later, I was drinking in a Stromness bar with a sailor, Billy Evans. He liked to quote the ballads of Robert Service, a Scottish–Canadian versifier who, in Orkney bars, was regarded as a serious rival to Burns. Suddenly Billy began to quote from Marvell's *Horatian Ode on Cromwell's Return from Ireland*.

> He nothing common did or mean
> Upon that memorable scene, . . .
>
> Nor called the Gods with vulgar spite
> To vindicate his helpless Right,
> But bowed his comely head
> Down, as upon a bed.

It is one of the great poems from the metaphysical anthology. The man who 'nothing common did or mean' is, of course, Charles I on the scaffold. Andrew Marvell himself had been on the Puritan side in the Civil War. A poem like his *Ode* is a fine illustration of the value of poets and poetry in a society. The great majority of people look at a situation with blinkered eyes, and are pleased that it should be so, because it makes life and thought easier and more tolerable. The imagination of the artist encompasses everything; 'He has', said Keats, 'as much delight in the creation of an Iago as of a Desdemona'. So Marvell saw the execution of the 'great tyrant', 'the man of blood', with pity and wonderment; and with delight that language could be compelled to the service of such deep mysteries, beyond the rivalry of kingdom and commonwealth.

✧ ✧ ✧

If I celebrate here, in plain prose, a young beautiful woman who lived in Edinburgh at this time, it is because she deserves to be remembered, and there is a danger that she may be inadequately dealt with if someone comes to write about the Scottish literary scene in the decade round 1960. The idea of the Muse who brings out the best in artists is ancient, of course. Some modern poets have their Muse, a woman who transfigures their work and guides them like a star, *stella maris*. This girl was actually called Stella. I met her one summer evening in The Abbotsford, together with someone else who has become a nameless shadow. But this girl with the sweet-smelling honey-coloured skin and the sweep of bright hair was delightful to talk to. She laughed a great deal – not the empty half-nervous spasmodic spillings of many young women, but out of a deep well of humour that was forever renewing itself. She thought, that first evening, that I was a fisherman. We didn't trouble to sketch in our backgrounds.

How long after that was it that she came to a party at the MacCaigs' house? I think it was one of the bigger parties where guests – some uninvited – kept dropping by with their 'cairry-oots'. But after midnight the tide of revellers began to ebb, until when the summer dawn started seeping through the Leamington windows there was no one left but Stella and myself. Even our hosts had gone to bed. I remember nothing of our dialogue but the laughter and delight of being in her company. At dawn Stella had run out of cigarettes – we spent a while looking here and there for a half-smoked one in an ashtray, or one forgotten in a packet. When the shops opened, I went out and bought cigarettes for Stella. It was a joy to give her things.

Stella would be necessary to this story, of course, because she awoke in me a delight I had not known before. But she had a wider richness. Charles Senior the Glasgow poet wrote a poem about her called 'The Muse in Rose Street'. The title describes her perfectly; it was on *poets* that this extraordinary girl cast her spell. It could almost be said that all the contemporary poets in Scotland were in love with her, at one time or another. That future Scottish literary historian will have a busy winter's work, discovering how much poetry was woven about Stella in the 1950s and 1960s.

She was very beautiful. She was intelligent, but not to the extent that it becomes a strain or a pose. She liked art and music and literature, but not sufficiently to make a kind of religion of it, as happens so often nowadays (for everyone must give allegiance to some 'reality' outside the cave of shadows that is oneself). What emanated from her was a kind of radiance, a rich essence on which poets and artists feed to sustain themselves. It is a rare mysterious innate quality, that cannot be acquired.

There was great happiness, simply to be with her: at Cramond, in her parents' garden at Juniper Green, window-gazing along Princes Street, drinking coffee in the Laigh or Crawford's, travelling in buses and trains.

Once, unexpectedly, she crossed over on the ferry to Orkney, and stayed for two weeks – it is a time (Easter 1962) of confused happiness and pain.

Stella was poor, as the world goes, but the wealthy patronesses of the arts had nothing to bestow like her gifts. (In actual fact she worked as a kind of receptionist in a photographer's establishment.)

She suffered, because of her endowments. Beneath the radiance and the serenity was a deeply vulnerable person. The passing sorrows of the world she was compelled to endure with a double or a triple intensity. She was open, to a dangerous extent perhaps, to the sufferings of others; she made instant instinctive response to a torn bird, or some old one too sick to do housework or shopping.

In this way, Rose Street was a dangerous environment for her. She drank, to begin with, because she loved people, and a little whisky put glancing edges on stories and talk and poetry. She drank, in the end, to dull the pain of life. She was so loved by so many in those taverns that her glass was rarely empty for long. Alcohol, that at first is a place of laughter and heightened sensation, becomes in the end a prison.

It is a sorrow to think of her and what she might have been. She had all that was necessary to be a good wife and mother, and a leaven in any community: not just a good neighbour, but such a neighbour as one might think of gladly on wakening: 'Stella will be hanging out her clothes . . . Stella will be speaking to the cat at the end of the street . . . Stella will be going to light poor old Mrs MacGregor's fire this morning, she being ill . . .'.

It was not to be. The sweetness that most women keep for husbands and children she gave to the poets of Scotland, and to the helpless and the suffering.

I write this in the middle of May, two days before her birthday which fell on the same day as Edwin Muir's (the 15th). They shared some characteristics: gentleness and compassion. But Edwin, being of an older generation, never met Stella.

For Stella's birthday, for years, I had always written an acrostic poem. And this year, 1985, I had written her birthday poem in good time, in February or March. She did not live to see this 15 May. She died, suddenly, in her Comiston flat a few weeks ago; but her health had been precarious for years. Somewhere in the great music, she is lost: but lost is the wrong word, of course. She wrote nothing herself, but what she truly was, her rare lovely unique essence, is a part of the literature of Scotland.

May it be well with her, who loved and suffered so much.

Birthday Poem: S.C. (15 May 1980)

Send
Today to
Edinburgh, fair greetings, and
Love, never
Lessening
As the years sere, awaiting snow.

Call together
All
Remembered sweets
That were, once, in the
Winsome sixties,
Roses at Juniper Green, the juniper (with lemon or tonic)
In Rose Street,
Gather,
Hoard in one dewy cluster, despatch
To Stella in Comiston.

Stella Cartwright (for her birthday – 15 May 1982)

So, once in the 50s
There was this crazy chap, high among clouds,
Edinburgh-bound.
Laurel-seeking he was, out of Orkney,

Long and salt his throat
Among the stanzas that starred the howffs of Rose Street.

Could he not bide forever in that beautiful city?
A sweet girl, one day,
Rose, a star, to greet him.
To him, she spoke sweeter than rain among roses in
                                          summer,
While poets like columns of salt stood
Round the oaken Abbotsford bar.
I, now
Going among the gray houses and piers of Stromness,
Hear that voice made of roses and rain still; and see
Through storm-clouds, the remembered star.

I studied hard, particularly near examination times, and
always passed. Only at weekends did I drink a lot. On
Sundays, no pubs opened, but there was then a strange law
in Scotland, whereby 'bona fide' travellers could be given
reasonable refreshment in certain licensed hostelries.
Strictly interpreted, to get a drink you had to be on a
journey from three miles or more away, *en route* to a place
at least three miles further on. So, on entering the hotel bar
in South Queensferry or Bathgate, you were presented with
a ledger and asked to sign your name, together with place
of setting out and place of destination. At South
Queensferry, we usually stated that we were on our way to
Bo'ness, an unlovely town on the Firth of Forth. ('Why
anybody would want to go to a place like Bo'ness on a
Sunday afternoon beats me,' said one of my friends,

signing the ledger.) Those 'bona fide' drinking places on the skirts of Edinburgh were, on Sundays, thronged with city folk. Occasionally, we would take a risk and drink in Edinburgh itself. ('If the police come in,' said Harry Taylor, a university librarian and one of our company of boon drinkers, 'plead guilty right away. You only get fined £2 . . .' But no long blue shadows ever fell across us.)

On the Monday morning, though often slightly hung-over, I was always ready and eager for study.

There must have been Orcadian 'moles' – Edinburgh had plenty of Orkney students who reported my tipplings back home. One day I got a letter from the Director of Education, John Shearer – the same man who had taught us science and maths at Stromness Academy – with a gentle warning in it. The Orkney Education Committee was disturbed by rumours. I was able to reply, blithely, that I had just come second in the English Literature class of 300 students. The guardians were seemingly appeased, for nothing more was said.

Very beautiful it is in Edinburgh in May and June. But June is the month of degree exams, and my memory of Junes in Edinburgh is of sitting in dark rooms while outside the girls went by in light summer dresses and long sun-tanned arms, and birds and flowers and foliage and children and clouds were making holiday, and even the old folk drifted here and there in a dream of peace. It was hard, on such days, to unravel the intricacies of *Beowulf* or *Gawain and the Green Knight*, and decide whether Shakespeare, in *A Midsummer Night's Dream*, or *Macbeth*, had meant the play to carry such or such a freight of meaning across the centuries. (Almost certainly he hadn't.)

The June of the final exams in 1960 was the most dark and punishing mill of all. It was, I think, a particularly beautiful month outside: I *had* to be outside. I sat, sulking and turning pages of text- or notebooks, under the trees in the Botanic Gardens.

The exams lasted a week. At the end of it I felt mentally bruised. I waited in Edinburgh till the results came out in July: I was awarded second-class honours like most of my classmates. My mother came down from Orkney for the degree ceremony in the McEwan Hall. Afterwards Norrie – my next oldest brother who was teaching English at Portobello, Edinburgh – and his wife Hazel entertained us to a meal in a good hotel. Edinburgh was a-flutter that day with black gowns. 'A proud day, a proud day,' said an elderly man as the four of us walked by, I in my hired gown and carrying the degree diploma in a red cylindrical box. Such is the Scotsman's reverence for learning. The day I wrote my first sonnet had been a much prouder day, and also the day I first laughed with Stella over one of the fine old oak tables in The Abbotsford in Rose Street.

✧ ✧ ✧

So, that was a four-year period in the desert of time used up: it had been a kind of bazaar of books, lectures, papers; of sitting and lingering and talking with a variety of people, many of them interesting, a few of them fascinating. In Stromness I had been one of the 'chorus of drinkers'. In Edinburgh I had joined a new 'chorus' – Sydney Goodsir Smith, Harry Taylor, John Broom, John Durkin, Stella Cartwright, Donald MacArthur, Ian MacArthur, Wilf MacLean, Peter and Jane Froestup, Stan Green, and a few others that came and went on the periphery. There were a few sore heads and guilt-hauntings, after particularly severe sessions; but, looking back, it was a time of delight and laughter.

Beyond this thronged bazaar that had kept me for four years, the desert waited; unless, that is, I found a job and settled down. For such as me, there was only one avenue open: teaching. Hundreds of students – many thousands, in the century of compulsory education – have gone into teaching, not out of any sense of vocation but because there is no other thing they can conceivably do. I enrolled, dully, at the Moray House College of Education in October 1960. There were lectures and tutorials of crushing boredom: I tend to think it was myself that cast the cold shadow. A woman gave us voice tests. A very old doctor looked over us briefly and passed us as fit, though at that time, looking back, it seems to me that my ancient ally the tubercle bacillus was hastening my way and may have been already in residence. At the end of a few weeks we who were to become teachers were sent out to schools in the vicinity, to see how we would perform in a teaching situation.

At that time I was living in the house of my friend John Broom in Bathgate. (Mrs Thomson had given up taking lodgers – time was eroding her formidable strength.) The Moray House authorities directed me to a new primary school called Boghall in Bathgate. Modern architects have much to answer for, but some of them at least have made schools that must be places of delight to children, and Boghall was one of them. I forget the name of the lady teacher who ruled the classroom I was sent to, but she must have been an excellent teacher, because her score of pupils – boys and girls – responded eagerly and happily to her teaching. I had little to do; I was sent to the back of the class, an observer. The usual variety of subjects was taught.

One day Mrs P. the teacher said, 'Boys and girls, I have to be away for half an hour or so. Mr Brown will be in charge of you. See that you behave well. Now just carry on with what you're doing . . .' For several days these model pupils must have been observing me, weighing me up, probing my armour for chinks. And now they had me to themselves. I never saw such an astonishing transformation. The little angels were suddenly little demons. They rose from their ordered desks and swarmed around me; I know I am wrong to imagine sneers, mockery, jibes. But I felt like an apprentice lion-tamer in a den of ferocious spitting lion-cubs. How long they baited me I don't know – it was a hideous time. At last Mrs P. returned, and they were gentle as doves again. She must have asked me how things had gone. I don't remember what I replied. But I knew then, with absolute certainty, that God hadn't called me to be a teacher. I was directed, horrified, to another Bathgate school, a Catholic senior secondary. I seem to remember numbing my mind with drink at the lunch-break, in a pub called The Fairway, with John Broom.

And then my ancient ally was suddenly there. I had a bad bout of bronchitis – so bad that I lay in bed in Bathgate for days, feeling wretched. One Saturday afternoon Stella came; somebody took a photograph of her sitting on the edge of my bed. I looked so ill in the picture that I tore it in two, so that Stella only appears between the straight margin and the ragged edge. I remember that John Broom had a party at the weekend, and I struggled out of bed and sent a shot of whisky through me. The sickness persisted; it grew worse. Dr Verney, the university doctor – an ex-rugger Scottish international, and a kind man – removed me to hospital, to the students' ward. X-rays were taken. I was sent on to Dr Crofton, the chest specialist, another very pleasant man. Dr Crofton showed me the X-rays, an old one and the present one, with a shadow on it; there was no doubt that the tubercle was active again.

I agreed to enter the City Hospital as a patient the following day. The next twenty-four hours were mine, to do with as I pleased. I started by drawing a lot of money out of the bank. Then I lunched off chicken, and whisky and beer, with a BBC producer called Robin Richardson in The Abbotsford. Then I went on a spending spree, mostly presents for Stella. At five I was back in the pubs. I drank deeply all evening. I found myself, late that night, in Stella's house at Juniper Green. Intensity of drink brings out some kind of nastiness in me; I woke up next morning and was severely censored by Stella's father Jack Cartwright, normally the mildest and most tolerant of men. I got to know, somehow, that Stella and John Broom were taking the train to Glasgow. I found myself in the same train, rekindling the dying embers with more whisky from the buffet. I remember taking a swipe at Stella with my foot on a Glasgow street, and two police-men looking back, debating whether I ought to be arrested or no. Stella and John Broom disappeared into a pub. I was alone and lost and very drunk in a strange city. With a drunkard's cunning I tracked them down. Now there was no losing me. John Broom disappeared, I think to some meeting, but possibly he was glad to shake off such a dangerous nuisance. Stella wouldn't speak. I managed to dog her to the station. I bought her a glossy magazine; we were friends again. I had lost my return ticket, and had to buy another, and between Glasgow and Edinburgh I lost that. At Waverley Station I paid for three fares. But the revelry was not over yet. I managed somehow to get to Milne's Bar. I remember one face in Milne's, Robin Lorimer the publisher, and it was shocked. At closing time I had to catch the last bus to Bathgate. I fell into a drunken swoon and woke at a place called Blackburn, some distance beyond; the conductress was shaking me. 'This is as far as we go,' she said. I enquired about Bathgate. 'Lucky for you,' she said, 'we're going back through Bathgate to Edinburgh.'

There was a letter from Dr Verney in the morning post, asking why I hadn't reported at the City Hospital – I must go there, at once . . . I spent a last hour of freedom in Milne's Bar. A friend called a taxi. I was delivered, bruised and badly hungover, at the City Hospital.

But in those days 'the elastic powers' were strong.

My lungs responded quickly to 'the miracle drugs',

chiefly streptomycin; the huge doses of PAS were, I think, replaced now by a couple of tablets a day called INAH.

There is a sanatorium at Deeside near Aberdeen called Tor-Na-Dee. In the days before National Health it had been an establishment for well-off tuberculous patients; now its stylish gates were open to all. (Further up the Dee was another sanatorium called Glen-a-Dee: there Somerset Maugham had been treated for TB in the 1920s or 1930s; he used it as a setting for his short story 'Sanatorium'.)

In 1960/61, a section of Tor-na-Dee was reserved for Scottish students. Every patient had a room of his own. Outside there were beautiful gardens, and, hidden by trees, the river.

But I almost forgot to tell of the train journey from Edinburgh to Aberdeen. John Broom had offered to keep me company. A guard took charge of me and ushered me into a compartment that had a notice in red stuck to the window of the door: HIGHLY INFECTED PATIENT: ENTRANCE FORBIDDEN. John Broom was only allowed in after a careful scrutiny. This notice put us in a hilarious mood for the journey north. We had bottles of beer to refresh ourselves. At Aberdeen another guard was waiting with a kind of spray-gun with which he thoroughly disinfected the compartment. John Broom and I almost fell over each other with laughter. An ambulance was waiting to take me the few miles to the hospital.

I spent a winter there, in great comfort, with visitors (including Stella) and books and writing paper. I was beginning to write verse again: dense tortured stuff. Occasionally in the afternoon, I took a bus to a pub in

Culter, a village up-river, or to another nearer the city kept by an Aberdonian who had been a professional footballer in England, though drinking was strictly forbidden to Tor-Na-Dee patients.

Nearly all doctors, in my experience, are good men. Dr Kay at Tor-Na-Dee liked literature, and was kind and considerate to me always, even on one occasion when I came back very late and a bit drunk from Aberdeen.

Officially, I was still a student. Some time in February 1962, patched up once more, I was put on the train to Edinburgh, where the portals of Moray House were waiting.

Soon after that, I wrote to the Principal that it would be better if I gave up all ambition to teach.

I returned to the beautiful desert of Orkney, but not for long.

✧ ✧ ✧

In those days – the early 1960s – there seemed to be plenty of money to spare for post-graduate study. I got to know about this, and applied, and was accepted to do a year's post-graduate work on Gerard Manley Hopkins. It would be honest to say at once that I chose Gerard Manley Hopkins because – apart from the imagist poet T. E. Hulme – Hopkins' collected poems are probably the fewest in English literature; and I had no intention of immersing myself in the immensities of Pope's *Essay on Man*, or Wordsworth's *Prelude*, or Spenser's *The Faerie Queene*, or

Pound's *Cantos*. It was essential to choose a writer of small output. But I had always loved Hopkins' poetry, and I was eager to know how he forged and hammered and welded those resounding marvels. The image that comes closest to Hopkins is that of a blacksmith, fettling 'for the great gray dray-horse his bright and battering sandal . . .'. No English poet ever fell upon the language with such skill, sweetness and boisterous daring.

It was a heroic lonely attempt to put song back into a language grown thin and washed-out. Somewhere literature had left the high road and smithy and market-place for the salon and the university, and grown anaemic.

It was necessary, Hopkins thought, to go right back to the beginnings, to rediscover a lost power and beauty. He strove to enter the first 'house of making', where word-men worked with all the excitement of men discovering ore in the rocks, and realising what marvellous artefacts could be made: crude, perhaps, but resonant with possibilities.

He strove to make himself one of the ancient smelters and smiths of poetry.

What he made was utterly new, and so had no place in the mainstream of late Victorian literature. The editor of the Jesuit magazine *The Month* took one perplexed look at the manuscript of 'The Wreck of the *Deutschland*' and sent it back to the poet–priest. What Hopkins produced was so new that it lay – a bundle of manuscripts – in Robert Bridges' desk for forty years before it was published. Then, in that time of new beginnings – Pound and Eliot – readers recognised an amazing originality. (The word originality, 'from the beginning', is appropriate; we tend to think of original work as having its face set towards the future. In great verse the language is 'before the beginning and after the end/And all is always now . . .'.)

But what was poetry for? The verse of any time faithfully reflects the spirit of the time.

In spite of the 'optimism' of Browning – that we can't help now but feel to be forced and a bit artificial; though no doubt, the man was sanguine and ruddy-cheeked – the poetry of Victorian England is suffused with a melancholy that darkens often into a settled despair. It can be felt, again and again, in the verse of Tennyson: *Maud* and *In Memoriam*. Even Browning was touched by the dark finger when he wrote 'Porphyria's Lover' and 'My Last Duchess'. But the poem that sums up the age best is Arnold's 'Dover Beach': 'the melancholy sad withdrawing roar . . .'.

No, cried Hopkins, poetry is for gladness, dewfall and childhood, 'innocent Maytime in girl and boy', it celebrates the ever-springing freshness of nature. Nature is an infinite feast. For look: we speak of grass, and falcons, and soldiers, and stars. But it is wrong, in a sense, to speak so generically – given our cast of thought, it is necessary to make such simplifications, but every blade of grass differs from the other infinite grass-blades; a falcon is not only different from every other falcon, it changes from second to second, splendours never on earth before flash from its pinions, as it turns in the changing light of a morning (and no two dawns are ever the same either); a Highland burn is superficially like streams and rivulets everywhere on earth, yet it is unique, new, changing with glooms and gleams and burn-music from moment to moment (and even when we say 'moment' it is an arbitrary measure and division of time, for the behaviour of the burn is outside time altogether, it is set in an altogether more marvellous framework). A soldier, a ploughman, a farrier – so we name such men and such trades – but who shall ever tell the richness and uniqueness of a soldier glimpsed in the street, Harry and his horses and plough cleaving the earth, Felix Randal between his forge and his anvil? A poet can faintly celebrate the mystery that is man – 'immortal diamond'.

Where does the glory come from, that streams forever through the firmament and the world of nature with its endless variety of creatures, and maintains them and keeps them in their courses, and has a keeping of them always, beginning to end?

It comes from God; the marvellous bounty comes from God and belongs to the glory of God: 'Glory be to God for dappled things . . .'. Thus Hopkins and his shouts of joy.

There was another Hopkins, the poet of 'the dark sonnets'. I have mentioned the melancholy of Victorian poetry; it is all pale gray shadows compared to the black pit Hopkins went to at a certain late period of his life, probably when he was teaching classics at University College, Dublin: 'I am at a third remove.' He was a stranger, and lost, hating himself and the piles of examination papers he had to correct, abandoned (it sometimes seemed) by God; or at least the comfort of God's presence was no longer felt.

Those five or six sonnets, magnificent as pieces of literature, are terrible documents. He feels himself exiled from

God's Kingdom; he is closed up in the lonely cold prison of himself. 'Selfyeast of spirit a dull dough sours.' He tastes crumbs of the bread of perdition. 'I see the lost are like this . . .' Such abandonment is all the more terrible for a man who is a priest; who holds in his hands every morning at Mass the Bread of Heaven.

Like Job, like the Psalmist, he complains. Why has the evil time come upon him? 'Why do sinners' ways prosper and why must/ Disappointment all I endeavour end?' It is not self-pity; it is a brave encounter with God, a wrestling, a desolate but stubborn questioning that must yield some kind of an answer. *Thy will be done.* But why in this particularly grievous and bitter way?

If there had been no God it would have been foolishness to dispute with Emptiness and Silence. But, whatever happened, he was not entirely abandoned. God was absent – the knowledge of absence was cruel – but his 'friend' might return. There was never any question of His non-existence: Hopkins had had too many proofs to the contrary. 'The world is charged with the grandeur of God.'

It was bitter, almost beyond words, but not quite. For out of the grief came the dark sonnets. Without The Word, that called all creation into being – the seven-syllabled word, whose last syllable is peace, completion, goodness, resolution – the words of the suffering poet could not come into being.

I have mentioned the healing aspect of poetry: the pouring in of oil and wine. Part of it comes from the work well-achieved: the poet himself, and all his readers and listeners, feel the wounds and the bruises (for we are born to trouble) but the pattern, the song, the dance more than make up for all. Without the Creator, the lesser creations of poet, artist, musician could not be.

We affirm as best we can 'in part', brokenly.

This is very ancient knowledge. Orpheus the great singer descended into hell, and 'drew iron tears down Pluto's cheek'.

No one knows, for sure, what anguished the soul of Hopkins all 'that year of now-done darkness'. He was one of those sensuous poets, like Keats and the young Shakespeare, upon whom sight, touch, sound, smell, taste break with all-but-shattering intensity and vividness: the whole body trembles with the assaults of beauty.

> When drop-of-blood-and-foam-dapple
> Bloom lights the orchard-apple
>   And thicket and thorp are merry
>   With silver-surfed cherry
>
> And azuring-over greybell makes
> Woods, banks and brakes wash wet like lakes
>   And magic cuckoocall
>   Caps, clears, and clinches all . . .

And yet he was a Jesuit priest, trained to a life of austerity and self-denial. In one of his early poems, 'The Habit of Perfection', he warns himself to keep a strict guard upon his senses. There is a perfection of being beyond the reach of the seductive five; the senses are but faint shadows, whispers, flavours of a perdurable reality.

Elected silence, sing to me
And beat upon my whorled ear,
Pipe me to pastures still and be
The music that I care to hear.

Shape nothing, lips; be lovely-dumb:
It is the shut, the curfew sent
From there where all surrenders come
That only makes you eloquent . . .

One element in 'the dark night' was the tension between
the sensuous man and the ascetic.

When he began to write again, as a priest, after years of
silence, he could reconcile the two. The rich swarming
never-exhausted beauty of the world: it was the garment of
God. The Holy Spirit spreads bright wings over the hills at
dawn. Christ and all His hallows are there when the harvest
stooks are brought in, and participate in the rustic song
and dance.

What is all this juice and all this joy?
A strain of the earth's sweet being in the beginning
In Eden garden . . .

In that dark year the ascetic quarrelled with the child of
nature – this is the only explanation I have – the austere
guardian turned on the pastoral poet suddenly and, curtly,
warned him to look to himself; weren't the beauties of
nature beginning to fade already? April was over, it was the
season of the sere, the yellow leaf; soon it would be winter.

This was the strange shy passionate tormented poet that I devoted myself to for two years at Edinburgh University. 'Devoted' is the wrong word. With idle delight I turned the few pages of Hopkins' *Collected Poems*, and also the astonished and not altogether approving notes of Robert Bridges at the end. I read his letters to Bridges, Coventry Patmore, and Canon Dixon (an Anglican priest–poet whose verses began to fade as soon as they were written). I made a serious attempt to understand his theories of prosody: sprung rhythm, outrides, instress, inscape, etc., without ever really understanding how he wanted his poems to sound. He would score a line here and there almost like music: thus and thus must the rhythm go, this syllable must be accented rather than that, from that beat the whole line takes life and energy and being. I tried again and again to follow the conductor (who ought to have known, surely, for he was the composer too) but I could not fit my voice to the stern eccentric beat. Now I don't worry about it – I read those lovely poems in my own way, often aloud, and it seems to work; in any case there's no one there to listen.

The long cruel winter went on and on – there seemed no end to the dark night. Spring returned to the world outside. 'Birds build, but not I build . . . Mine, O then lord of life, send my roots rain.'

He died in Dublin, aged 45, of typhoid. It is said, his last words were, 'I am so happy, so happy . . .'

'Inscape in the poetry of Hopkins': that was the subject of my post-graduate study. After two years with the poet I was not quite sure what this most famous of his technical

For the Islands I Sing

innovations was exactly . . . I read not only Hopkins himself on the subject, but the scholars and critics who have burned midnight candles working it out, defining and elucidating. Inscape? It is related somehow to 'landscape'. It is the 'scape' inside a man, the sweep and range and mind and spirit, the diversity and abundance and flow and fall and aspiring that, seemingly so various, are yet a unity. But this inner 'scape' does not exist by and for itself; it is balanced, held in a sweet tension and harmony by the lovely world outside, the 'scape' that is always changing as the man moves here and there in space and time, himself a centre of infinite horizons, always questing, never satisfied.

Complete thy creature dear, o where it fails . . .

If I had had to write a thesis on Hopkins, I would have wrestled more mightily with him, and would have written some black tome to please examiners. But I wasn't asked to write a thesis. All I had to do was write some notes on some aspect of the poet that took my fancy, and hand it in to Miss Winifred Maynard. She and I got on well, but I know that she did not think much of my thoughts on Hopkins. 'There's no need to write essays,' she said. 'Make notes, let me see those.' But I couldn't make notes. I was much happier fixing on some idea or image and writing cursive sentences and paragraphs, and rounding it out to some kind of conclusion. Whatever the ideas and the treatment, they failed to cause any stir of excitement in Edinburgh University. Somewhere in a cupboard upstairs

157

my Hopkins essays still lie in manuscript, unread for years, sheathed in cobwebs. From time to time someone will say, 'What happened to your work on Gerard Manley Hopkins?' And I answer, 'Some day when I'm an old man in the Eventide Home I'll take it out and blow the dust off and put it in order for a publisher . . .' It might indeed be interesting some day to read again my thoughts on Hopkins from a quarter of a century ago – I'm sure I would have to agree with Miss Maynard that my appraisal is not good enough. I'm sure no publisher would give those fugitive essays a second glance. Nor would I want them read by others.

During those two years when I dallied with Hopkins – for it was dalliance rather than the wrestling of the serious student – I stayed first at Leslie Place in Stockbridge. There a Glasgow writer called Edward Gaitens rented a basement flat, and he sub-let a room to me. Years before, Edward Gaitens had had a book of short stories published by Cape, called *The Sailing Ship*. I was very much impressed by the title story and two other stories in the collection. Later, Edward showed me a novel he had had published, *The Dance of the Apprentices*, which I did not like. The craft of writing is in many ways a sad business; it is unlike such trades as carpentry or mason-work where, having learned the rudiments, a workman can only get better with time. For the writer, the wind bloweth where it listeth. Many a young darling of the Muse is deserted by her, or kept severely at a distance. It seemed to have been that way with Edward Gaitens. He had grown up in a poor Catholic area of Glasgow, and he was one of those boys who respond quickly to idealistic Socialism and the beauties of nature and art. He refused to be conscripted in the First World War, and was sent to prison for his courage. In 1962, when I first met him, he was ageing and his health was poor; especially he suffered with his stomach. His two books had been published a while before – *The Sailing Ship* had been praised by H. G. Wells. I think his gift had deserted him, but he kept still a bright eye and an eager spirit, and he was working on a radio play, tapping for hours on his type-writer, or sitting beside the one and only luxury in his spartan room, a really good radio, listening to music. He had long abandoned Catholicism, but men must be believing something and Edward's religion was art.

I had to pass through Edward's room every morning to make my breakfast in the kitchen. Edward's breakfast was very strong cups of tea.

We got on well enough. There were one or two little rows that quickly passed. Mostly we 'had words' about literary matters. Sometimes, when I got my post-graduate cheque, I would take Edward out for a drink. No beer or whisky for him; spirits burned inside him like a red-hot poker. His eyes glittering with delight, he would slowly sip a Dubonnet and smoke cigarettes.

When Stella visited me in my room, I took her next door to meet Edward. Like many another writer, he was at once under her spell.

Stockbridge is a pleasant part of Edinburgh. It must have been a little country village at one time, until the expanding city crept all around it, waves of houses, and engulfed it. And yet, in the 1960s, it kept its own identity – it had never allowed itself to be completely whelmed.

The room I lived in was dark and dingy. The fire in the grate burned erratically and sometimes filled the room with dense smoke. The first time that happened, the window was jammed and a joiner had to be sent for.

Edward's sleep was often interrupted by an old couple in the next flat who fell to quarrelling in the middle of the night; and then Edward had to beat upon the wall. I heard all about it next morning, bringing to his bed a cup of hot black tea. He had those flashes of anger.

I think Edward would have been happy in the artistic world of *fin de siècle*. The decade of the 1960s belonged to the young. It was hard for him, being old and poor and ill and neglected.

Once while I was staying in his flat he had a marvellous holiday. In his First World War prison there had been another conscientious objector, an idealistic well-off man. He was dead, but his widow lived on and remembered Edward. One post delivered to him a cheque from this good woman for £75 or so – an amazing wealth for a pensioner then – and an invitation to stay at her place in London. While Edward was away, I had to sit in the dingy waiting-room of some foetid office and pay Edward's rent, about which there was some complication, a kind of misunderstanding between factor and tenant . . . Edward flew home from his holiday in London 'with magic in his eyes'. It was a night of terrible storm – the plane had been blown about the skies – but Edward was so happy that he didn't care much what happened.

He had spent all the £75 in one happy splurge.

He has been dead for more than a decade now (as I write this).

I am pleased to know that he is not entirely forgotten. Anthologies of Scottish stories include his work. Only a week ago I was sent a collection called *Streets of Stone*: Glasgow stories, in which 'The Sailing Ship' and 'Growing Up' appeared.

One coincidence: Edward Gaitens had been a mature student at Newbattle too, but that was after my time, when Edwin Muir was dead.

✧ ✧ ✧

A few writers came to Orkney between my time at Newbattle and at Edinburgh. One was Ian Hamilton Finlay, who was then living with his first wife in Rousay. At that time he was writing short plays for radio, and short stories. He had enthusiasm for the literature of the north, particularly Scandinavia. He wrote some beautiful short stories. But he won fame later for his 'concrete poetry', and for his garden in Dunsyre, Lanarkshire, with its poems inscribed in stone.

He had stories published in the weekend pages of the *Glasgow Herald*, edited by Anne Donaldson. He encouraged me to send some of my work to her, and she accepted poems and stories.

One day a slight fair young man called on me. He was a marine biologist on a fishing research ship, berthed for a weekend at the pier in Stromness. His name was Burns Singer, and though I had never heard of him until then, it was no long time before he let it be known that poetry was his true vocation. He was no slight lyric poet; he liked working on large canvases, so to speak – on large spaces of silence. Some of his long poems had appeared in a thick luxurious-looking magazine printed in Italy, *Botthege Oscure*, subsidised by a wealthy noblewoman. The very week that he was in Orkney, a huge poem of his appeared in *The Listener*, 'The Transparent Prisoner'. He was totally self-assured; he had not the least doubt about his vocation and talent. He had been brought up in Glasgow, of Polish–Jewish and Irish ancestry. Dedicated artists are not universally accepted. In the few days that he was in Orkney, I saw how Burns Singer roused moderate men to outrage. I got on well with him myself, as we drank beer and spoke of poetry in the bar of the Royal Hotel. He tossed off lyrics with careless ease; he showed me a poem written to a girl in Shetland, casually met: 'Her Cigarette'. He strolled into the *Orkney Herald* office in Kirkwall where I was then working and hammered out a sonnet on the typewriter and dedicated it to me. Edwin Muir told me that Burns Singer would phone him and recite poems he had just written. 'I think he is a good poet,' said Edwin.

Burns Singer had high admiration for Hugh MacDiarmid, and wrote an article on him in *Encounter* called 'Red Eminence': a piece that drew a cold reply from MacDiarmid himself. He had visited MacDiarmid and his wife, and it seems they hadn't got on very well. Valda MacDiarmid kept faithful and constant vigil over the poet's peace; no doubt his privacy, even in his lonely cottage near Biggar, was being constantly broken into.

Burns Singer praised Dylan Thomas to the sunrise and to the stars. 'If his intellect had been equal to his imagination, Dylan Thomas would be among the very greatest poets,' he said to me.

Having made a few friends and a few enemies in the course of that weekend, the poet–biologist sailed away. He took a few of my latest poems with him; thanks to him, one appeared in *Encounter* (the first sonnet in *Loaves and Fishes*) and the other, 'Elegy for Thorfinn', in a literary magazine whose name I forget.

His memory lingers in my mind, pleasant, bizarre, stimulating. Once, years later, at a party in Edinburgh – I was not present – someone must have mentioned me in a slightly derogatory way. Singer, who was present, rounded on the man and lashed him with his tongue – 'You are speaking about a good friend of mine.'

He died suddenly, while still a young man.

A few years ago, when I was reviewing poetry for *The Scotsman*, Burns Singer's *Collected Poems* was sent to me.

I would like to have been able to say good things about it, but those poems are the most difficult and opaque I have ever wrestled with. There must be merit in them, possibly great merit, but I can't see it. I did not review the book.

Contact with writers like Finlay and Singer, and their stimulation and help, kept the flame burning.

After Edwin Muir left Newbattle, he spent a year as the Charles Eliot Norton Professor of Poetry at Harvard. He wrote to me from time to time, long letters written with those early ballpoint pens that left blue gouts and smudges on the script. He had, he told me, shown three or four of my poems to the literary editor of *Harper's Bazaar*. In due course those thick glossy magazines reached me, crammed (I seem to remember) with advertisements for ladies' clothes and cosmetics; but with poems and other literary pieces in the fairways between. And soon after appeared the cheques, that took away my breath with their extravagance.

The estate of literature is full of petty rages and back-biting jealousies. It is fair to say that there is a good deal of practical encouragement and kindness too. Without the help of other poets, I might have remained an obscure Orkney writer; or if not, any wider recognition would have been delayed for years perhaps.

✧ ✧ ✧

I had come back from university to Mrs Thomson's bed-sitter one afternoon in 1958, to find a letter from the Hogarth Press. Norah Smallwood, a director, had been shown a selection of my poems by Edwin Muir, and she said she would like to publish them. I exulted, silently. I had never dreamed that such a thing could ever be. Many authors have a heart-breaking heroic time of it hawking their manuscripts from publisher to publisher before they fall on good soil. (Most manuscripts of novels and poems are for flames and the dustbin.) It would be interesting to know how many good books in manuscript vanish without a trace, after the last publisher's door has been closed against them. There must be a few, certainly. What bitterness it must be then, for an author, out in the cold with a work that he knows to be good! It happens more frequently, perhaps, in the world of art than in literature. A week or two ago, I watched on television one of Van Gogh's lesser-known paintings being auctioned in America. Only the wealthiest people had been invited to the sale (the catalogues were very expensive). There they sat, sleek and scented, gross with oil profits and real-estate profits, going up the golden ladder with negligent nods of the head and flicks of the hand. The painting, of a scene from Van Gogh's asylum window, was sold for – I think – nine million dollars. 'Lord, what would they say/Did their Vincent walk that way?' . . . In his lifetime, he had sold one painting for a few francs. Had Vincent shown up, he'd have been thrown down the steps of the auction hall for a tramp.

Thanks to Edwin Muir, my entry on the literary scene couldn't have been easier. The book of poems, *Loaves and Fishes*, came out in 1959. The reviewers gave it a cool reception. I wasn't looking for raptures, but I was a bit hurt by John Wain's brief notice in – I think – the *Observer*, in which he said that the poems had been influenced by Edwin Muir. In fact, no two kinds of poetry could be more different. Muir adventures deep and far into the racial memory, and the treasures of image and symbol he brings back are steeped in the purity and light and tranquillity of the beginning. My poems have a much narrower range in time – a thousand years maybe – and they celebrate as best they can 'whatever is begotten, born, or dies', generation by generation, until they stop with memories of my father and his letters and tailor's shears. I find it impossible to write about the Orkney of oil and uranium deposits. It seems too that the people of my generation, though much better off materially than their grandfathers, have lost a richness and strength of character. The twentieth century has covered us with a gray wash. Newspapers and cars and television have speeded up the process. It could not be otherwise. There are few lonely untouched places on earth now. The seeming affluence may be temporary and uncertain, after all.

It is the modern world that provoked Edwin Muir and me into poetry. His adolescence in Glasgow, his 'expulsion' from Prague in 1948 when the Communists took over; those dreadful experiences he set against his childhood in Orkney. Without that contrast, he would have been a different kind of poet, and a lesser one.

I hadn't experienced such wreckages in my life; rather, the slow seepings and rottings of the new age. But here we must be careful. The new age, though it carries in one hand the cup of poison, brings in the other the benefits of science. Without the 'miracle drugs', streptomycin and PAS and INAH, I might have died some time in the 1950s. I don't think, either, that I would have written much beside a fish-oil lamp, in one of those old crofts that still exist as museum pieces here and there, with pigs grunting and hens fluttering behind the peat-fire in the centre; and a dame-school a mile or so away where I might have gone to learn reading and writing. Yet that was a time, 150 years ago, when life was dangerous and the language rich, and the community was invested with a kind of ceremony. The people lived close to the springs of poetry and drama, and were not aware of it. I draw any art I have from great-grandparents, and further back; I acknowledge the gift and the debt, but I would not have wished to live their hard lives.

I got together a new group of poems in 1962 and sent them to the Hogarth Press. It often happens that a second book is not as good as the first. The manuscript was returned, and in due course came a letter from Cecil Day Lewis, the poetry editor, saying that among other faults the poems had 'outcrops of barren imagery'. I was disappointed at the time, but, looking back, I am glad that collection wasn't accepted. It is to taste bitter enough fruit, to be forced to read again, ten or twenty years later, poems that I exulted in when the ink was still wet on the page.

Day Lewis's rejection spurred me on to better things. I remember a period of a month or two when new poems homed in on me, sometimes one every day; and I knew at once that they were better than the rejected lot. Cecil Day Lewis accepted them – though he had reservations about a few, especially a group at the end that nowadays I cannot bear to let my eyes fall on – and a second book of poems called *The Year of the Whale* appeared in 1965. It was well received by most of the reviewers.

Of late years I have come to place small value on reviews, favourable or unfavourable or lukewarm. Many intelligent readers set great store by them, and seem to be waiting to see what reviewers say before they have an opinion of their own. Of course it is pleasant to get a good review, if the reviewer shows that he has tried to understand what he has read. But often it seems to me that a writer is praised for the wrong things and blamed for the wrong things; in which case both praise and blame are meaningless. I have often wondered, with novel-reviewing, how the reviewer can possibly have read the four or five novels he is writing about, in a comparatively short time, and discovered the essence. I think it was James Agate, who used to review books in the *Daily Express*, who said he rarely bothered to read the whole book, because he could always tell a good horseman by the way he went up to his horse.

By the mid 1960s, I had written a cluster of short stories. I sent them to Norah Smallwood and she accepted them at once. They were published in February 1967 as *A Calendar of Love*. Some of the stories in that book were written at great speed and hardly touched afterwards. The title story seemed to unfold in that way, except for one bitter lonely scene that I patched together at last with desperate third-rate 'poetical' prose. And one of the little episodes in the story 'Five Green Waves' took years before it could be stitched invisibly into the whole. But stories like 'The Troubling of the Waters' and 'The Seller of Silk Shirts' came easily and naturally; and 'Jorkel Hayforks' also.

People who bother to comment on my poems and stories mention how often the number seven occurs. It is a mysterious and beautiful number in itself, and it occurs often in nature and in ceremony: the colours of the spectrum, the continents, the days of the week (the seven-syllabled Word of Creation), the deadly sins and the cardinal virtues, the ages of man, the family ('seventh child of a seventh child'), as if every family, whether it has three children or twelve, yet yearns towards the good number seven); the five loaves and two fishes of the miracle; the sorrows of the Blessed Virgin.

In the making of a story or a poem, the number seven has extraordinary power. The writer can look at a character, or an event, or a place from seven different viewpoints. It is obviously impossible to hope to grasp and hold a totality; art imposes a pattern on the endless flux. My particular pattern is the heptahedron.

I have relied often on the seven-faceted poem or story. Once a character suggests itself (or a situation, or an episode) to the imagination, it is caught and held in the mystery of the number seven, and there it is imprisoned till the song or the fable is finished and it is free to go, like Ariel.

I am wary of straying outside the charmed circle of the seven, but often the demands of story or play or poem force me into a ten-sectioned or twelve-sectioned work: but even then I feel sure that the fruitful number, the seven, is dominant, and dictates the whole tone and structure.

A Calendar of Love got extraordinarily good reviews. Meantime, between the sending off of the typescript and publication, other stories had been written. They appeared two years later: *A Time to Keep*. It got even warmer applause than *A Calendar of Love*.

Oases were appearing ever more frequently. It seemed as if my days in the desert might be nearly over.

Meantime, in my literary innocence, I had done something questionable – the publisher Victor Gollancz had asked me to write a book on Orkney for £200 (plus royalties, of course). I agreed at once. At that time I was still poor, and £200 was a lot of money.

A kind of superior guide-book did not appeal to me. I think I had read *Brendan Behan's Island* – an enchantingly funny book – and it suggested a more imaginative and varied approach, with plays, poems, fragments of history, and real characters in it. I relied heavily on *Orkneyinga Saga*, especially the episodes of the Battle of Clontarf, the martyrdom of Magnus, the Viking Crusade of 1151–54; but of course I let my imagination work on them, and it may be that I wrenched history too far out of its frame. For example, I don't know whether the Stations of the Cross was a part of Catholic ceremony in the twelfth century – and being lazy, and averse to research, I didn't bother to enquire – but I make Earl Rognvald and his fellow voyagers follow the Stations of the Cross in the Church of the Holy Sepulchre in Jerusalem. I think Eric Linklater questioned that part – and also the Rackwick Stations – when he reviewed the book in the *Guardian*. But, looking back, I think I achieved an imaginative wholeness, especially as each Station has a sea-image. Christ is the young hero–skipper guiding his ship into the rage of history.

As a kind of coda to the chapter on Magnus, I wrote a play about two old tinkers – a man and his wife, the woman blind – going to the tomb of the dead earl in the bishop's church (Orkney's first cathedral), on the tidal island off Birsay. Later I cast the whole Magnus story in a play called *The Loom of Light*. Later still it became the novel *Magnus*, sections of which I think to be among the best writing I have done. Few readers agree with me. But it's always like that, I think. 'What thou lovest well' is often looked at coldly by others.

There was a chapter on Rackwick, and one on Robert Rendall, and a great Tolstoy story – 'What Men Live By' – made into a play and given an Orkney setting.

The drawings in the book are by Sylvia Wishart, she who restored one of the old Rackwick croft houses from imminent rot and decay – North-house; she spent weekends and holidays in the valley, painting. Sylvia's parents lived next door to my mother in Stromness. We knew each other well, and had spent many happy days in the valley.

An Orkney Tapestry, published by Gollancz, came out in the same year as *A Time to Keep* (1969), and it too was well received.

During the writing of *An Orkney Tapestry* I had slight qualms, and I must have written to Norah Smallwood telling her what was afoot. She was not altogether pleased, and had no hesitation in telling me so, and Gollancz too. I ought to say here that apart from one or two ruffles on the surface, I enjoyed Norah Smallwood's friendship till she died in 1984. She was all that a publisher could be to a writer at the beginning of his career, gently guiding and cherishing and encouraging. Soon after *A Time to Keep*, Norah suggested that I should try my hand at a novel. I didn't think I was capable of such long-distance running. Simple heptagons: I could manage them well enough – never the labyrinth of a novel. Still, I had a notebook at home with a few pieces of dialogue and stage direction in it. I had imagined an island in Orkney with a little fishing village at one end. The characters were rather crudely sketched in, in the 'flat' Dickensian mode. Each scene depicted an ordinary day in the life of the village, with the villagers intermingling like instruments in a piece of chamber music. There were the shop-keeper and his wife; three fishermen of whom one was a religious fundamentalist, one a many-childrened alcoholic, and one a long lazy man who neglected his fishing in order to write a history of the island from the Marxist point of view; a young handsome ferry-man without scruple or conscience; the schoolteacher from Edinburgh who, slowly withering like the apples in her bowl, is hopelessly in love with the ferryman; the laird and his horse-faced sister (a dispenser of high-handed charity) and their beautiful teenage niece who comes on holiday and is smitten too by one look from the ferryman; a girl with several illegitimate children, their names all beginning with 'S', who loves everybody and everything and bears no grudges; a down-and-out beachcomber who spends his National Assistance money on meth; a retired sailor, and his sister who keeps hens; the young minister who drinks spasmodically and in secret, and his guilt-stricken mother; the inn-keeper whose inn is slowly tumbling about his ears. To give another dimension to this flat village, an Indian pedlar arrives in the island, selling silk articles (such Indians were common in Orkney before and just after the war), and he looks on this common Orkney place from half a world away – eastern airs and spices waft from him. In addition to the villagers, there are the various island farmers and their families, and the school playground is boisterous with children. But there is something sinister about this village – not in itself, it is a kind of tawdry gossipy Eden – but it is threatened from without by some nameless anonymous pressure which it will not be able to withstand or resist. What this destructive power was, I had no idea when I scribbled out the little pieces of dialogue into a grubby notebook.

Of course Orkney had, twice in the early part of the twentieth century, experienced vast irruptions into its pastoral life-cycle – the outpouring of troops and ships in the two world wars; populations here and there had creaked and cracked under the pressure. A few merchants had prospered well: torrents of gold poured through their tills. Farmers had had to leave their ancestral fields at short notice to make way for military emplacements and runways. Young Orkney men sailed away to their death in France or in the air or in Atlantic convoys. But those incursions lasted for only a year or two; the tide ebbed, leaving ugly concrete scabs here and there that had been camp sites and gun-and-searchlight emplacements; and a high-water fringe of money where the flood had lapped.

It was something vaguely like this – preparations for a third world war, much more hideous than its two predecessors – that I imagined as the destroyer of the village and the island.

I wondered if those fragments of dialogue and slow dance could be made into a novel. I made a start, tentatively, and the novel began to take shape and assert itself; it slowly broke through the chrysalis and something strange and new began to emerge. Again, it was to have the

heptahedron form: the seven days of the week. I don't
know how it is with other people, but with me every day
from Monday to Sunday has a distinct aura and flavour: I
think memories from childhood have a lot to do with it –
the washing-day smell of Monday, the agricultural air of
Wednesday (which brought the farmers and their wives in
to Stromness, to the mart), the wild sweet freedom of
Friday when we burst through the school gate for the
weekend, Sunday with its stillness and unction like a white
marble tombstone. In the novel, *Greenvoe*, I tried to give
each day a distinct tone by changes in the weather. This is
no fake contrivance either, because visitors to the islands
are astonished by the swift alternations of storm, stillness,
rain, sun, sea-haar; sometimes a single day has three or
four kinds of weather. You can see a raincloud trailing its
fringes across the horizon, between blazes of blue and
gold, on many days of the year.

Most of the characters remained 'flat', true (I think) to
the dynamics of the book: it was impossible to look deeply
into them all. But one character emerged and began, in her
shy self-effacing way, to assert herself: Mrs Elizabeth
McKee, the minister's mother. It is a strange experience for
a writer, when a character claims independence for herself,
like Mrs McKee: not complete independence of course, but
as if she said, 'I won't be confined within two dimensions,
there are other facets of me that must be shown, I refuse to
be an inert paper cut-out.' And so Mrs McKee, whom I
grew to love more and more as the novel unfolded, led me
gently into her past life; and, wisely, she led me among
places I was familiar with: Edinburgh, and chiefly the dis-

trict of Marchmont where both of us had lived at different times. Also she led me into places of the mind that I knew a little about, those places of guilt, prosecution, judgement, which, while they last, make life bitter and terrible. One endures, somehow – a little light comes in, and grows – and one wakes from the dark dream with a few syllables of thankfulness. But one knows that the evil time will return, sooner or later.

I think Elizabeth McKee and I have had more joy and understanding of each other than any other character I have imagined. When I say 'imagined', I mean a richness and resonance. Existence is so mysterious, especially for an artist, that the shapes of his imagination can be more real than most of the living shadows he nods to in passing on the street every day. The creators of great characters – Shakespeare, Tolstoy, Mann, Forster, Molière – are more than puppet masters: they have seen that every individual – even 'the living shadows' passing on the street, seemingly empty and without meaning – are 'diamond, immortal diamond'. T. S. Eliot, for all his genius, fails in this respect: human beings for him are always 'men and bits of paper, whirled on the cold wind'. The union of 'the fire and the rose', at the end of *Four Quartets*, is meaningful in religious terms, like the transfiguration of 'poor patch, matchwood' into 'immortal diamond'. But the slow smoulders and cracklings of human life have been bypassed in his work.

I have imagined Elizabeth McKee, and I am content with her.

I have often been asked: what in *Greenvoe* is the irresistible power that finally breaks the island and the village? That it is some kind of advanced missile base or early-warning system is the usual conclusion. But I have left it vague, purposely. At the time *Greenvoe* was being written, there was no word – if there was, I never heard it – of North Sea oil. It was certainly a year or two before the first probes were made for the uranium ore in which areas of Orkney are rich. I sometimes fob off people who demand an answer by saying that, at the time, there was a menace in the air, one could feel the chill of some huge on-coming shadow. But probably all I meant was that material progress, which had been coming anyway with ever-accelerating momentum, would end by ruining the life of Orkney as we know it, and all the other unique lonely places of the world beside. 'Black Star' was simply one monstrous symbol of dispersed forces and currents and tendencies which, for more than a century already, had been undermining an ancient way of life. The deserted village of Greenvoe is Goldsmith's Auburn, and Rackwick, and the Forest of Arden, and the little town by river or seashore of 'Ode on a Grecian Urn'.

Greenvoe had, on the whole, a favourable reception. One or two reviewers sneered at it as a crude imitation of Dylan Thomas's *Under Milk Wood*. But while it was being written, I had never given a thought to *Under Milk Wood*.

It has proved to be the most popular of all my books, with an American edition, translations into Swedish and Norwegian, a Penguin edition with several reprints, a schools edition and a braille edition. And now, as I write, there is talk of making it into a film for television.

As for me, I do not care to turn its pages any more. I quickly grow cold to what I have written. Occasionally, over a glass of whisky, I take *Greenvoe* off the bookshelf and commune for half an hour with my friend Mrs McKee. She is a consolation. We have things we can say to one another.

✧ ✧ ✧

I think I should end the story soon. There is nothing much further to tell, except that books were published at fairly regular intervals: the novel *Magnus* in 1973; a poem-cycle about Rackwick, *Fishermen with Ploughs*; more books of short stories and books for children, beginning with *The Two Fiddlers*; two collections of articles that I wrote weekly for the local newspaper *The Orcadian*; *Winterfold* and *Voyages* (poems); a novel last year (1984) that should really have been called a fable, for it eschews realism and works in the stuff of fantasy, *Time in a Red Coat*. It was not received with rapture, yet there are episodes in it that I am glad to have written, like the meeting on a Napoleonic battlefield of a press-ganged Orkney soldier and the mysterious ageless girl who carries with her through many centuries the healing gift of art, and also a bag of Chinese coins to solve more immediate problems – the imaginative and the practical are impotent without each other; together they can bind up the most terrible wounds. I am particularly pleased with the Orkney soldier's lingering at the crossroads between Life and

Death, uncertain which to choose, at last setting out on the easy road to oblivion through all the preceding scenes in the fable until recalled at the last moment by the voice of woman – mother and sister and bride – who carries in her hands the jar of love, compassion, and healing without end.

The relationship between men and women is often explored in my work, and the tendency always is to associate men with what is dangerous, exploratory, breaking open and casting down, and women with endless waiting, patience, consolation: Veronica and the women of Jerusalem have their places on the Way of the Cross. The women of Orkney wait through the centuries for the men to come back from the fishing in the west, or from longer journeys, the Greenland whaling and the penitential voyage to Jerusalem. And often all that they find is a broken oar in the ebb, or bright hair meshed in the seaweed.

In the novel *Magnus* there is another chapter I am glad to have written. Re-telling the story of Magnus and Hakon is well enough; but quite suddenly one morning, as I was thinking of ways to tell the story of the actual martyrdom in Egilsay in 1117, it occurred me that the whole story would strike a modern reader as remote and unconnected with our situation in the twentieth century. The truth must be that such incidents are not isolated casual happenings in time, but are repetitions of some archetypal pattern; an image or an event stamped on the spirit of man at the very beginning of man's time on earth, that will go on repeating itself over and over in every life without exception until history at last yields a meaning. The life and death of Magnus must therefore be shown to be contemporary, and to have a resonance in the twentieth century. I did not have far to go to find a parallel: a concentration camp in central Europe in the spring of 1944.

Magnus appears as Pastor Bonhoeffer (or another like him) and is executed in circumstances and by people compared to whom the twelfth-century Norse killers perform with a ritualistic inevitability: there is a kind of tragic beauty, even, in what they do, far removed from the hideous slaughter-houses of the Nazis.

I know little about the concentration camps other than what I have read casually in books and newspapers, or seen on film. I used to reproach myself with being too lazy to research a situation thoroughly before writing about it. But now I am sure that this is not how the creative energies work. All that is required is a suggestion, a flavour, a rhythm, an aroma. The imagination seizes on such intangibles and creates upon them living forms that are more real than a first-hand account by the best journalist – I was tempted to say, than history itself, but the reality of history and the reality of literature are quite different, each being one facet of the truth.

If ever I have attempted to research a background to some story I was getting ready to write, I have found that the spirit of the story was always crushed under accumulated facts and figures. I know it is not the fashion nowadays for novelists and playwrights to work in this way, with intangibles and the free play of the imagination. They must go and see for themselves, taste the salt of a strange sea or catch as well as they can the rhythms and intonations of an exotic dialogue. Something in the spirit of modern man demands this, the factual more emphasised than the imaginary. If so, laziness and timidity and distrust of 'the real' have left me stranded centuries back. I can only appeal, very humbly, to the great spirits of the past. Was Homer ever in Troy? Did he sail on a wine-dark sea? Nobody has ever discovered that Shakespeare was in Venice, or Elsinore, or Scotland. Was he 'pricked for a soldier', ever, or sailed westward into an unknown sea? Yet the very air of Scotland, it seems, saturates *Macbeth*. The salt and the splinterings of shipwreck are everywhere in the opening of *The Tempest*.

The fact that the historical characters in Shakespeare – Theseus, Julius Caesar, Richard II – wore contemporary Elizabethan dress, and spoke the language of the streets and the court, demonstrates an instinctive wisdom concerning the archetype and its repeated patterns through history; the Elizabethan writers did not have to reason these things out, they felt them in their bones. Realism is the enemy of the creative imagination.

A corollary is that any small community is a microcosm. It is not necessary to stray very far from your back yard. The whole world gathers about the parish pump. But stories from under the horizon ought always to be welcome – and so they have been, in Orkney, for centuries: but the stories are never utterly new.

There are mysterious marks on the stone circle of Brodgar in Orkney, and on the stones of Skarabrae village, from 5,000 years ago. We will never know what they mean.

I am making marks with a pen on paper, that will have no meaning 5,000 years from now. A mystery abides. We move from silence into silence, and there is a brief stir between, every person's attempt to make a meaning of life and time. Death is certain; it may be that the dust of good men and women lies more richly in the earth than that of the unjust; between the silences they may be touched, however briefly, with the music of the spheres.

Appendix
(November 1993)

This autobiography was written in 1985.

There is nothing much to add.

Age makes erosions here and there, in mind and body. One forgets names. The sight dims (I had a cataract operation in the winter of 1988). Malignancies appear (I had a cancer operation in 1990).

Writing becomes a greater joy. Reading becomes more difficult because there is such a torrent of new books. I tend more and more to read the books and poems that have pleased me through the decades: Tolstoy, Waugh, Forster, Brecht, Mann, Greene, Eliot, Muir, *Orkneyinga Saga*.

Television is a kind of anodyne – I have to be careful to look and listen only to programmes I think I might like; not politics, not pop music. The turning of great books into television drama is nearly always a failure: *The Mayor of Casterbridge, Scarlet and Black*. Dickens is the sole exception.

I have largely lost my taste for drink. John Barleycorn

has turned his back on me. 'Not before time,' I can hear some of the old Hamnavoe women say in the kirkyard.

An old man becomes ever more reclusive. He is glad to meet old friends and talk about half-forgotten things (the actual events becoming, with each telling, more and more like legend). At a deeper level there is the fable Edwin Muir speaks of. Deeper still, and one begins to participate in very ancient ritual.

But new friends have appeared too, from time to time, a matter that Samuel Johnson was grateful for, in his day, and so am I.

It is good, I know, to hear music in a way our forebears didn't know, by means of radio, tapes, records. There is occasionally the uneasy thought, that there is something suspect about playing the same Beethoven or Mahler recording over and over – something anti-life, in spite of all the beauty. Oughtn't music, and poetry, to be a spontaneous thing, like the old country fiddler reaching for his fiddle, and the story-teller gathering listeners about him at the fire? Then each reel and each tale differed in every performance, the tremble of life was in it . . .

Sleep changes its pattern in old people – five hours at night instead of eight – but then a shallow wave goes over in the afternoon, on the couch.

There are new fears, too. Twice in recent years, rats have got into the house, and given gloom and anxiety for a few days until the scratching behind the skirting ceased . . . In childhood and later, such things caused no distress. Then, too, there was a joy in storms, the hay-stack levellers and the ravelled roof-slates. Now I feel uneasy as the growl in the gale's throat deepens. The huge enchantment of snow is a burden to an old man; the only way he can enjoy it is to write of early or imaginary snowfalls.

The failure of state socialism in Eastern Europe is a sobering matter, especially if you conclude that the only alternative is such capitalist societies as America. Nearly every intelligent young person is a socialist, and has looked to the future with shining eyes; surely it is possible, certainly desirable, to establish the good society. Stalin and Mao had shining innocent eyes, too, aged twenty. What is never taken into account is what we thought a barren priest-crafted superstition, the Fall of Man. There will never be a good society, there are too many flaws in human nature. At best we can keep society from being wholly evil, with Belsen and the Gulags. Even as I write this, terrible things are being done by neighbour to neighbour in Bosnia, Burundi, Haiti, South Africa. In spite of universal education, in spite of parliamentary democracies, 'the devil goes about as a roaring lion'.

State socialism may not have worked, so far. But the idea of the good society ought always to be in our minds. 'Market forces' bring the jungle to Bourse and Stock Exchange.

Terrible diseases are well on the way to cure; then an unknown disease like AIDS spreads like a stain over the continents.

Old men have to contend with noise. On the few occasions I go to bars, I am often driven out by the juke-box. Even in such quiet places as hospital, the background music seems to be acceptable to nurses and patients.

After all my experiences of hospital, I dread going into such mindless noise; I ask to be put in some corner without TV or radio. Workmen on the street have transistors going. I grew up in a world of silence acceptably broken by wind and sea, the gossip of old women at close-ends, the noises of fishermen and tradesmen at their business; I live in age in a world of clamour and endless babble, and am glad only that I don't have to endure these things in a great city.

An old man withdraws into a narrower circle, just as in November the light lessens.

Getting up in the morning is still not too much of an effort; I can still make toast and egg and tea; my friend Brian Murray comes in and lights the fire; my friend Surinder Punjya does my shopping. Renée Simm, the Dixon family and the Bevan family see to it that I don't starve.

After breakfast, the happiest time begins, when I take down the writing paper and pen, and begin where I left off yesterday at noon. This year more poems than ever have come, 'heptahedrons' or seven-leaf poems. I think a few of them are as good as anything I have done. The imagination is still working, and the tools of the workshop are bright with use.

But all casts its shadow, even things considered good. For two decades Wordsworthian hauntings, Hopkinesque angsts, have visited from time to time, and then for a week or more there is a depression to be endured. So severe it can be that one longs for oblivion, even when at the same time one knows that it is right that it should be so – it is fitting one should have to share one's transient suffering with an AIDS patient, or a child lying with a bloody stump of a leg in some shell-broken hospital in Sarajevo . . .

This is a hard kind of justice, laid on one's shoulder, that we should be glad to bear. An easier way is to enter, ritually, into the sufferings of people and nations; and here justice becomes meaningful and comely; but most people nowadays will have nothing to do with that. Christ opened himself to the worst rejection, pain, and desolation. In the Mass the sacrifice is repeated, over and over, every second of every day, all over the world; but Golgotha is made beautiful and meaningful by 'the dance of the altar', the offering of the fruit of people's labour as they themselves journey to death, suffering and rejoicing: the bread and the wine.

It is the wayside inn where we stay awhile for refreshment and rest. 'Love bade me enter . . .'

The simplest Mass is the most beautiful event imaginable.

The scriptural Passion that was its matrix is beyond the imaginative reach of Dante, Shakespeare, Tolstoy. We ought to know, instinctively, that it *must* have happened that way: '"Beauty is truth, truth beauty – that is all/Ye know on earth, and all ye need to know . . ."'

I think everyone, if he or she thinks about it at all, is aware of two wills at work. The personal will seeks security and power and love and success. There are strong minds with distinct aims in view that can carry a person a fair distance along the road of heart's-desire; but there are always accidents and imponderables that turn the stern face another way. Before 1789, would not Napoleon Bonaparte have been content with a captain's insignia? In an Elizabethan playhouse, what happened when a manager said one day to the country boy from Stratford, 'Here, Will, you have a way with words. See if you can patch up this old play somewhat'?

There is I think another will that we have no control over. A shaping divinity takes over from our rough-hewings. It 'prevents us everywhere', as Eliot says, but it also offers opportunities beyond anything we could have hoped for. We are hardly aware of the daily operatings, but looking back over one's life there are, it seems to me, clear evidences of this shaping spirit, whose 'preventings' we might have resented at the time; and, whenever it opened good new prospects for us, we attributed them to luck, or, more dangerously, to strengths and subtleties in ourselves that we were not aware of: we think then of ourselves as masters of our fate.

Great power corrupts absolutely, in part because the man of destiny thinks at last that the source of power rises from his inherent merits. But one of the most powerful men of modern times, Napoleon, could admit that the Paternoster is a transcendent sublimity: 'Thy Kingdom come. Thy will be done. Give us this day our daily bread . . .'

To lose one's own will in the will of God should be the true occupation of every man's time on earth. Only a few of us – the saints – are capable of that simplicity.

We are all one, saint and sinner. Everything we do sets the whole web of creation trembling, with light or with darkness. It is an awesome thought, that a good word spoken might help a beggar in Calcutta or a burning child in Burundi; or conversely. But there is beauty and simplicity in it, sufficient to touch our finite minds.

I say, once a day at least, 'Saint Magnus, pray for us . . .'.

Index

Index

Index

Index